CityPack
New York

KATE SEKULES

Adopted New Yorker Kate Sekules writes about travel, food and fitness for many magazines, including The New Yorker, Travel & Leisure, Health & Fitness, Food & Wine *and* Harper's Bazaar. *She is also a co-author of Fodor's* New York City, *author of* By Night: New York, *and a consultant on the US Mobil Travel Guides.*

City-centre map continues on inside back cover ◄

AA Publishing

Contents

About this book

KEY TO SYMBOLS

✚	map reference on the fold-out map accompanying this book (see below)	🚌	nearest bus route
✉	address	⛴	nearest riverboat or ferry stop
☎	telephone number	♿	facilities for visitors with disabilities
⏰	opening times	✋	admission charge
🍴	restaurant or café on premises or near by	⬌	other nearby places of interest
Ⓜ	nearest underground (subway) train station	❓	tours, lectures or special events
🚆	nearest overground train station	➤	indicates the page where you will find a fuller description
		ℹ	tourist information

ORGANISATION

CityPack New York is divided into six sections to cover the six most important aspects of your visit to New York. It includes:

- The author's view of the city and its people
- Itineraries, walks and excursions
- The top 25 sights to visit – as selected by the author
- Features on what makes the city special
- Detailed listings of restaurants, hotels, shops and nightlife
- Practical information

In addition, easy-to-read side panels provide extra facts and snippets, highlights of places to visit and invaluable practical advice.

CROSS-REFERENCES

To help you make the most of your visit, cross-references, indicated by ➤ , show you where to find additional information about a place or subject.

MAPS

The fold-out map in the wallet at the back of the book is a comprehensive street plan of New York. All the map references given in the book refer to this map. For example, the Chrysler Building, on Lexington Avenue, has the following information: ✚ E6 – indicating the grid square of the map in which the Chrysler Building will be found.

The city-centre maps found on the inside front and back covers of the book itself are for quick reference. They show the top 25 sights, described on pages 24–48, which are clearly plotted by number (❶ – ㉕, not page number) from south to north across the city.

NEW YORK
life

Introducing New York

What's that neighbourhood?

Almost every ten square blocks of Manhattan has a name.

Battery Park City
An official new neighbourhood, around the World Financial Center

Chelsea
The west teens to twenties; a gay male mecca and (way west) gallery land

Clinton
The city's uncatchy original name for Hell's Kitchen

Curry Hill & Row
Hill is E27th Street (Park/Lexington Avenues), Row is E6th Street (First/Second Avenues)

Diamond Row
Orthodox Hasidic Jews forge jewels here: W47th Street (Fifth/Sixth Avenues)

East Village
The name slapped on the tenements across town by bohemians priced out of Greenwich Village

Flatiron
A fairly recent recasting of the former photo district, and newish restaurants of Park Avenue South

Garment District
Where the garmentos roam: 28th–42nd Streets, around Seventh Avenue

Girl Ghetto
Cheap rent; east of Second Avenue, north of 68th Street

Vendors plying their trade on the city streets

Although you've heard so much about New York and seen it in countless films, you don't really appreciate it until you've had the experience. Then, when you finally find yourself in the middle of it, it's never what you expected.

A zig-zagging drive downtown from the Triborough Bridge, en route from JFK airport, will immediately show you the skyline, the Empire State, Times Square, Fifth Avenue and Central Park – a guaranteed thrill. But it is the unexpected quirkiness of the city that you cannot know until you see it. The proliferation of shoe menders' shops; road repairs with tall cylinders in the middle of the street belching out clouds of steam; the friendly geometry of fire escapes and the primitive silhouettes of water towers on roofs – these things characterise the city. As you make your first explorations, consider the early immigrants and how it was for them, especially those who were herded through Ellis Island, then crammed into Lower East Side tenements. Imagine how daunting the cast iron-framed SoHo buildings must have appeared to someone from say, Vienna. Although they are now scenes of costly loft living, homes to chain stores or swank galleries, during the immigrant boom, they were sweatshop skyscrapers – symbols of hope for a fresh future.

Today, the city is dwarfed by the World Trade Center's 107 storeys instead of the 'Cast Iron Historic District' of SoHo, which now appears human-sized. But New York's awe-inspiring first time effect still works – not through the big buildings, but through the lives inside them. Manhattan is built on a vortex magnetic to those who thrive on adrenalin and even chaos, and New Yorkers seem to move faster than anyone else on earth. Here everyone's in your face, everyone has an opinion, everyone has to deal with the difficulties of inhabiting this expensive crazy place. It is after your first glimpses of the skyline that you will make your first real acquaintance with the city, as you interact with people. You may find you get a taste for it. You may want to do it all again.

The Manhattan skyline from the Empire State Building

Gramercy
Since the 1830s, when the Park was laid out

Greenwich Village
Probably the most famous neighbourhood of all

Hell's Kitchen
Midtown, way west. The name was coined late last century

Ladies' Mile
Big shops lined Broadway from Union to Madison Squares in the 19th century, hence this anachronism

Little Italy
Virtually reduced to one street: Mulberry, Spring to Canal

Murray Hill
Home to J P Morgan, and all 'the 400' – Lady Astor's crowd: 34th–42nd Streets, First–Fifth Avenues

NoHo
'North of Houston' – a few streets around Lafayette

Nolita
'North of Little Italy'; the main drag is Elizabeth Street – all trendy, tiny boutiques

SoHo
'South of Houston' was the first made-up name to stick

TriBeCa
The 'Triangle Below Canal' is all lofts and restaurants

Turtle Bay
Sutton and Beekman Place between 42nd and 59th Streets – super-exclusive since the 1920s

NEW YORK IN FIGURES

Demography
- Population New York City (NYC): 7.3 million (including Manhattan population: 1.5 million)
- Average prison population: 18,736
- Catholic New Yorkers: 43.4 per cent
- Jewish New Yorkers: 10.9 per cent
- Baptist New Yorkers: 10.7 per cent
- Decline in murders since 1993: 60 per cent
- Decline in overall crime since 1993: 41 per cent

Geography
- New York City area: 301 square miles (including Manhattan area: 22.7 square miles; 13.4 miles long by 0.8–2.3 miles wide)
- Miles of streets: 6,400
- Miles of subway track: 722
- Miles of waterfront: 578
- Acres of parks: 26,138
- Number of skyscrapers: 200
- Average annual rainfall: 47.25 inches
- Average annual snowfall: 29.3 inches

Tourism
- Number of visitors in 1998: 34 million
- Number of international visitors: 6.04 million
- Number of hotel rooms: 63,000
- Hotel occupancy rate: 81.3 per cent
- Number of licensed taxis: 11,787
- Number of old chequered cabs: 8

Leisure
- Number of restaurants: 18,000
- Number of art galleries: 400
- Number of Broadway theatres: 38
- Number of Off-Broadway theatres: 300
- Average Midtown traffic speed: 5.3mph

Cab statistics

There is a fixed number of New York taxis, though with cab driving being a traditional occupation of newly arrived immigrants the driver population changes constantly. In 1993, 1,694 new licences were granted – though not to the 29 per cent of applicants who failed the English proficiency test. At the last count, there were 85 different nationalities among New York taxi-drivers, with 60 languages spoken, but no guarantee of geographical fluency – the knowledge of Manhattan required is rudimentary.

NEW YORK PEOPLE

WOODY ALLEN

Since he has one of the world's best-known faces, it's very strange actually to see Woody, and you do see him, sooner or later. "I can never leave," he has said. Woody shares an unspoken pact with New Yorkers. Everyone knows not to stare at him, not at the Gramercy Tavern or Elaine's, not at a Knick's game at the Garden, not even when he's on stage playing the clarinet, not even with Soon Yi by his side. In fact, the Soon Yi-gate scandals of 1993 did remarkably little to taint the love his home town lavishes on the guy who made the neurotic, hypochondriac Upper East Side *mensch* into a world-wide cliché.

DONNA KARAN

One of the few fashion designers to command movie-star-level recognition – at least of her name – Karan (emphasize the first syllable) came to fame well over a decade ago with a capsule collection of clothes for women over 20 based on a garment that has become the staple of every wardrobe, everywhere: the 'body'. Launching her 'DKNY' diffusion range widened the scope of this astute businesswoman and welded the idea of her clothes to the image of New York forever, leading some to suggest that she pay royalties to the city. See her 20-storey mural at Broadway and Houston and decide for yourself.

DONALD TRUMP

You think you've heard the end of Donald, and then he starts up another scheme or marries another blonde. A former pet project, Trump Tower, the vulgar pink and gold block on Fifth Avenue, is pure frozen 1980s, but the 1990s have treated this highest-profile wheeler-dealer OK too, after a shaky start. The shaky start left him in debt to the tune of $8 billion, with $975 million of it personally guaranteed. Somehow, he came out with the Plaza Hotel (though Citicorp share the control), his Taj Mahal gambling arena in Atlantic City, the Trump International Hotel and Tower at Columbus Circle, and his most recent development, Riverside South.

Woody Allen

New York types

Gay Life

This is one of the best cities in which to be gay, with a thriving, pulsating community for both genders. Whether quietly absorbed into mainstream life or visible through the information and support organisations, gay men and women are now firmly established in New York's social landscape.

Personal trainer

The gym boom is waning, as many journey inwardly to do yoga and qigong, but this hasn't affected the 2:1 trainer-to-New Yorker ratio. A trainer is mentor, guru, scourge and savior in one, and has been custom designed for NYC.

Panhandler

It's a sad fact of life in the city that you will see more homeless people than you can count. Competition for New Yorkers' dimes leads to some irresistibly inventive lines.

A Chronology

Pre-16th century	New York and the surrounding lands are populated by Native Americans.
1524	Giovanni da Verrazano makes the first sighting of what is to be New York.
1609	Henry Hudson sails up the Hudson seeking the North West Passage.
1614	Adriaen Block names the area 'New Netherland'.
1625	'Nieuw Amsterdam' is founded by the Dutch West India Company.
1626	That colony's leader, Peter Minuit, buys Manhattan Island from the Native Americans for $24-worth of trinkets.
1664	'Wall Street's' wall fails to deter the British, who invade and rename the island 'New York', after Charles II's brother, James, the Duke of York.
1763	Treaty of Paris gives British control over 13 American colonies.
1770	Battle of Golden Hill: Sons of Liberty vs. the British.
1774	New York 'Tea Party' – tax rebels empty an English tea clipper into New York harbour.
1776	American Revolutionary War begins. British HQ in New York. Declaration of Independence read at Bowling Green in July.
1783	Treaty of Paris ends war.
1785	New York is named capital of the United States.
1789	George Washington is sworn in as first US president at Federal Hall.
1790	Philadelphia is named capital of the United States.
1797	Albany takes over as capital of New York state.

1807	Robert Fulton launches his first steamboat, establishing trade routes along which many New Yorkers' fortunes lie.
1827	Slavery in New York is abolished.
1848	Start of first great immigrant waves.
1861	Civil War. New York joins the Union cause.
1868	The first 'El' – elevated train – opens.
1869	'Black Friday' on Wall Street.
1886	The Statue of Liberty is unveiled.
1892	Ellis Island opens.
1904	The IRT line opens – New York's first subway.
1929	The stock market crashes; the Great Depression begins.
1930	Chrysler Building finished – world's tallest.
1931	Empire State Building finished—world's tallest.
1933	Prohibition ends. Fiorello La Guardia becomes mayor.
1954	Ellis Island is closed down.
1964	Race riots in Harlem and Brooklyn.
1973	World Trade Center finished – world's tallest.
1975	New York is bankrupt. Saved by federal loan.
1987	Stock market crashes.
1990	David Dinkins, New York's first black mayor, takes office.
1993	Terrorist bomb damages the World Trade Center.
1994	Mayor Giuliani takes office.

People & Events from History

John Pierpont Morgan

John Pierpont Morgan

Banker J P Morgan (1837–1913) did everything with his money from founding the Pierpont Morgan Library (► 55) to saving New York – in 1907 he and the US Treasury bought $25m of gold to rescue the city from bankruptcy. His millions arrived with European investors in New York's 19th-century boomtime. He fielded those fortunes and watched over the founding of the US Steel Corporation.

TAMMANY HALL AND 'BOSS' TWEED

Tammany Hall was dedicated to fictional Iroquois chief 'St Tammany', in a spoof on the kind of upper-crust fraternities William Marcy 'Boss' Tweed and his cronies despised. A famous and typical Tweed extortion was the construction of the New York County Courthouse, which cost the city $14 million – $2 million for the building, and $12 million for the Tweed Ring. Bribery was routine for them. They bought votes with jobs and cash, and tried to buy – for $500,000 – the City Hall clerk who eventually turned them in. Tweed escaped from jail and fled, but was apprehended by Spanish police who recognized him from the Thomas Nast caricatures the *New York Times* had persisted in running. Altogether, the Tweed Ring defrauded New York of some $200 million.

NEW YORK FORTUNES

Certain names, enshrined in street names, foundations, and cultural institutions, are inescapable in New York.

John Jacob Astor (1763–1848) was a baddie. In 1834, he started investing the fortune he'd made in the fur trade in high-rent slums, squeezing pennies out of tenement dwellers while kissing up to high society. This made him the world's richest man at his death. The best thing he did was found the Public Library.

Andrew Carnegie (1835–1919) emigrated from Scotland, began as a cotton worker, and amassed vast fortunes through iron, coal and steel, ships and rail. Self-interest was not Carnegie's motivation. The $2 million for Carnegie Hall was the least of his gifts – libraries, trusts and charities benefited from his belief that to die rich was to die in disgrace.

Cornelius Vanderbilt (1794–1877) 'Commodore' Vanderbilt started with a ferry and ended with $105 million, which made him the richest American of his day. He converted the Staten Island Ferry into a steamship empire, then diversified into railways (► 36). After his death, his son Cornelius (1843–99) continued to prosper and doubled his money.

NEW YORK
how to organise your time

ITINERARIES

The best way to do New York is by not trying to see everything. You'll be so confused and exhausted, you'll miss what makes this a truly great city – things like the pace, the people, the chutzpah, the sights between the sights. In this spirit, the following itineraries are offered as guidelines for hanging a holiday on. If you do Itinerary Four on a Monday, Wednesday, Friday or Saturday, get off the bus at Union Square to pick up lunch from a Greenmarket stall (➤ 32). Saturday is ideal for visiting SoHo's galleries, although the Village will be swarming; avoid Sundays. For Itinerary Three, avoid Mondays as all the doors will be closed.

ITINERARY ONE	LOWER MANHATTAN
Morning	Ellis Island (➤ 26). Statue of Liberty (➤ 25). Brooklyn Bridge (➤ 29).
Lunchtime	Battery Park City (see panel opposite).
Afternoon	South Street Seaport (➤ 27). Walk through Financial District to:
Sunset	The World Trade Center (➤ 28) on West Side or Brooklyn Bridge on East Side.
ITINERARY TWO	MIDTOWN
Morning	Museum of Modern Art (➤ 38). Rockefeller Center (➤ 37).
Lunchtime	Grand Central (➤ 36).
Afternoon	United Nations HQ (➤ 51). Walk through Midtown to Macy's (➤ 71).
Sunset	Empire State Building (➤ 33).
ITINERARY THREE	MUSEUM MILE
Morning	Metropolitan Museum of Art (➤ 44).
Lunchtime	Central Park (➤ 40).
Afternoon	Whitney Museum of American Art (➤ 42). Frick Collection (➤ 41).
Sunset	Across the park to Lincoln Center (➤ 39).

ITINERARY FOUR	**UPTOWN—DOWNTOWN**
Morning	Solomon R Guggenheim Museum (➤ 45). Cooper-Hewitt Design Museum (➤ 46).
Lunchtime	Bus M1, 2, 3 or 18 down Fifth Avenue to Astor Place.
Afternoon	Greenwich Village (➤ 31), SoHo galleries, SoHo and Nolita shopping (➤ 45, 56 and 70).

The Empire State Building

Battery Park City

Battery Park City is still being built on 92 acres of landfill along the Hudson, but is almost finished now. Cesar Pelli's World Financial Center forms a part of it, but you may care to explore the residential areas of this futuristic city-within-a-city, especially the Esplanade (off Liberty Street) – over a mile of waterside stroll (or running track, as you'll see), with fine views of the harbour and New Jersey.

WALKS

INFORMATION

Distance 3 miles
Time 3 hours
Start point World Trade Center
➕ A12
🚇 N, R, 1, 9 Cortlandt Street
End point Greenwich Village
➕ B9
🚇 1, 9 Christopher Street/
Sheridan Square

Brooklyn Bridge walkway

DOWNTOWN HIGHLIGHTS

Turn your back on the twin towers of the WTC, pass Century 21 department store to your left on Cortlandt Street, and head north up Broadway. As you approach City Hall Park on the right, look left just past Barclay Street for the Gothic 'Cathedral of Commerce', the Woolworth Building. Still on Broadway, City Hall followed by the Tweed Courthouse comes into view on your right.

Walk east through the park and catch a vista of Brooklyn Bridge. Continue north up Centre Street. You now come to Cass Gilbert's gilt-pyramid-crowned US Courthouse on Foley Square at the south-east corner of Federal Plaza on your left, the neoclassical New York County Courthouse past Pearl Street on the right, then, past Hogan Street, the Criminal Courts (The Tombs).

Another block, and here's gaudy Canal Street, which you follow east to Mulberry Street (for more of a taste of Chinatown, take a detour around this area). Continue north up this artery of Little Italy (you'll need an espresso – Caffe Roma on the corner of Broome Street is recommended), and veer west on Prince Street. After two blocks, you're in the Cast Iron Historic District of SoHo. Look at the Little Singer Building (above Kate's Paperie) opposite as you cross Broadway. Take any route you please west through the cobbled streets of SoHo, heading north on any of these from Mercer to MacDougal to cross Houston Street. Three blocks later, you reach Washington Square, the centre of New York University.

Fifth Avenue starts at the north side. Look at gated Washington Square Mews (first right), turn left on W8th Street (see MacDougal Alley, first left), and right onto Avenue of the Americas (Sixth Avenue). On the left is the crazily turreted Jefferson Market Library. Keep heading west and follow your nose to Greenwich Village (➤ 31), perhaps stopping for lunch at Mappamondo ✉ 11 Abingdon Square

Live window display, Macy's

MIDTOWN'S GREATEST HITS

Madison Square Garden, behind Penn Station as you exit the subway, is not a garden at all, but a concrete cylinder for sports and concerts. Head two blocks uptown, then take 34th Street east one block to Herald Square, Macy's and Manhattan Mall. Toward the end of the next block, look up to your right. You're underneath the Empire State Building.

Head north up Fifth Avenue. Six blocks brings you to the *beaux-arts* magnificence of the New York Public Library, with Bryant Park behind. Go east on 42nd Street until you reach Grand Central Terminal, and on the south-west corner of Park Avenue is the Whitney's outpost in the Philip Morris Building. After a look in the Terminal (the Oyster Bar or one of the newer restaurants can provide refreshment), continue east a block and a half and on the left you'll see the Chrysler Building. Circumnavigate the Terminal, hitting Park Avenue again at 46th Street, with the MetLife building at your back.

A few blocks north you'll find the precursors of the Manhattan skyline: Lever House (north-west of 53rd Street), and Ludwig Mies van der Rohe's Seagram Building (east side, 52nd–53rd Streets). Go west on 53rd Street, south on Madison Avenue to 50th Street, and veer west. Here's Saks Fifth Avenue and St Patrick's Cathedral, on the right. Straight ahead is the vast Rockefeller Center. If you have energy, the nearby Museum of Modern Art could wrap up your tour.

THE SIGHTS

- Madison Square Garden
- Macy's (➤ 71)
- Empire State Building (➤ 33)
- NY Public Library (➤ 34)
- Bryant Park (➤ 58)
- Whitney at Philip Morris (➤ 42)
- Grand Central Terminal (➤ 36)
- Chrysler Building (➤ 35)
- MetLife Building (➤ 51)
- Lever House, Seagram Building (➤ 51)
- St Patrick's Cathedral (➤ 52)
- Rockefeller Center (➤ 37)
- Museum of Modern Art (➤ 38)

INFORMATION

Distance 3 miles
Time 2 hours
Start point Madison Square Garden
✚ C7
🚇 1, 9 34th Street/Penn Station
End point Rockefeller Center
✚ E5
🚇 B, D, F 47th–50th Streets/Rockefeller Center

EVENING STROLLS

INFORMATION

Museum Mile
Distance 2 miles
Time 1–2 hours
Start point 96th Street
✚ H2
🚇 6 96th Street
End point Fifth Avenue at Central Park South
✚ E5
🚇 N, R Fifth Avenue

The East Village
Distance 2 miles
Time 1–2 hours
Start point Houston Street
✚ D10
🚇 F Second Avenue
End point Greenwich Village
✚ B9
🚇 A, C, E, B, D, F, Q W4th Street

Park Avenue

A STROLL DOWN FIFTH AVENUE

If it's summer, you may wish to start in the early evening – around 6PM—and add a Central Park preamble, using the entrance just north of the Metropolitan Museum of Art (Met) at 85th Street, and perhaps watching the softball on the Great Lawn. Otherwise, start on Lexington Avenue at 96th Street, now a perfectly safe neighbourhood, but by no means as swanky as the one you hit once you head west. This section of Park Avenue is called Carnegie Hill, and from here on this walk takes you through Manhattan's most expensive and desirable zip codes. When you reach Central Park, turn left down Fifth Avenue and just gaze at the fantastic façades, many of them still private homes. Another half-dozen blocks, and there's the magnificent Met, then the Frick appears, followed by the fabulous Romanesque-Byzantine style Temple Emanu-El ✉ 1 E65th Street, one of the world's largest synagogues and home of New York's oldest Reform congregation. Don't miss that round window.

THE EAST VILLAGE

Coming up from the subway onto Houston Street by Second Avenue is not an aesthetic experience, but as you take off north, you'll quickly get the feel of this land of the hip. In the past few years, this former haunt of the demi-monde has almost lost its edge, though this has the advantage of supplying the visitor with a bottomless array of bars, restaurants, intriguing shops and happening cafés. That block of 5th Street to the west is where exteriors for the *NYPD Blue* precinct are shot; the next block, 6th Street, is filled with identical Indian restaurants with Christmas light decor. St Mark's Place (8th Street) is the nerve center of the neighbourhood. Go east one block to see sweet, dog-centric Tompkins Square Park, entirely surrounded by restaurants and bars (come back for a thorough exploration of Alphabet City – Avenues A to D were once no-go areas). Go west and see how the punk funkiness gives way to student pseudo-hipness as you reach the environs of New York University.

ORGANISED SIGHTSEEING

The classic way to orientate yourself and get an eyeful of the skyline is to hop on a **Circle Line Cruise** ☎ 212/563 3200 that circumnavigates Manhattan for three hours, accompanied by a commentary. Pricier, shorter, but more dramatic, is a helicopter tour from **Helicopter Flight Services** ☎ 212/355 0801, which scrapes the skyscrapers for 12 to 21 minutes. In between these extremes are the bus rides organised by **Gray Line** ☎ 212/397 2620, which include Trolley Tours on replicas of 1930s trolleys, and many standard bus-ride-with-commentary orientation trips. **New York Doubledecker** ☎ 212/967 6008 ferries you around town in a transplanted scarlet London double-decker bus.

A Circle Line cruise boat

For those who prefer to walk, many of Seth Kamil and Ed O'Donnell's **Big Onion Walking Tours** ☎ 212/ 439 1090 are gastronomic odysseys. But this entertaining duo also offer things like the 'Riot and Mayhem' tour of civil unrest sites. Another personalised, neighbourhood-crunching operation is **Adventure on a Shoestring** ☎ 212/265 2663, which have been leading small groups of walking tours for over 20 years. **'Wild Man' Steve Brill** ☎ 718/291 6825 leads maybe the most surprising tours of all – around the Manhattan wilderness areas, with folkloric and ecological asides.

If you want insight into the arts, there are a few backstage tours available, although Broadway theatres no longer allow punters into the working areas. The **Metropolitan Opera** ☎ 212/769 7020 has one-hour and half-hour tours by reservation and **Radio City Music Hall** ☎ 212/632 4041 offers a Grand Tour Behind the Scenes. **Art Tours International** ☎ 212/239 4160 do a similar sort of thing with art, scheduling visits into the studios and lofts of actual artists. **Mainly Manhattan Tours** ☎ 212/755 6199 conducts a literary tour of 'New York Left Bank', visiting the Greenwich Village homes – outsides only – of literary luminaries like Eugene O'Neill and e e cummings.

EXCURSIONS

Brooklyn Heights

INFORMATION

Start point Grand Army Plaza
+ Off map at G14
🚇 2, 3 Grand Army Plaza

Prospect Park
☎ Recorded information:
  718/788 0055

Boathouse Visitor Center
🚇 D, Q Prospect Park
☎ 718/788 8549

Brooklyn Botanic Garden
✉ 1000 Washington Avenue
☎ 718/622 4433
🕐 Apr–Sep: Tue–Fri 8–6; Sat,
  Sun 10–6. Oct–Mar:
  Tue–Fri 8–4:30; Sat, Sun
  10–4:30
🍴 Café
♿ Good
🎫 Free

Brooklyn Museum
✉ 200 Eastern Parkway
☎ 718/638 5000
🕐 Wed–Sun 10–5
♿ Good
🎫 Inexpensive

A BIT OF BROOKLYN

A separate city until 1898, this 71-square-mile borough of well over 2 million souls is intimately connected to Manhattan, yet it is different – as even a superficial exploration proves.

Exit the subway at Grand Army Plaza, a vast oval roundabout dominated by the Arc de Triomphe-like Soldiers' and Sailors' Arch, which functions as gateway to Prospect Park. Designers Olmsted and Vaux felt this park, opened in 1867, was better than their earlier Central Park. Inside is near-rural woodland and meadow, and the exquisite Brooklyn Botanic Garden with its Elizabethan Knot Garden, its Japanese Garden, its Conservatory and the Fragrance Garden with braille signs for the blind. Park Rangers give tours of the entire park, departing from the Boathouse.

On the park's north-east corner is the Brooklyn Museum. Intended by McKim, Mead & White to be the biggest museum in the world, it has turned out to be the seventh largest in the USA, with collections from pre-Columbian to 58 Rodin sculptures, and what's considered by many the best Egyptian collection outside the British Museum (and Egypt).

You shouldn't ignore the rest of Brooklyn, but it's a big place.... For a flavour, stroll around leafy, middle-class Park Slope, north-west of the park, and around Brooklyn Heights south of the bridge for great Manhattan views.

STATEN ISLAND

Many Staten Islanders would like to secede from the city – why should they share New York's problems and taxes, they argue, when they not only have their own discrete, rather rural community, but are also completely ignored by all four other boroughs? Whatever their political status, however, their island is pure pleasure to visit, especially in summer when all kinds of events are held. Once you've enjoyed the famous ferry ride, buses are the best way to get around.

Snug Harbor is a work in progress – a visual and performance arts centre in an 80-acre park of 28 historic buildings. Long established here are the Children's Museum and the Botanical Garden, as well as a couple of performance venues and a restored row of Greek Revival houses. Both this and historic Richmondtown have a programme of summer fairs, concerts and other events. In the exact centre of the island, Richmondtown traces 200 years of New York history through restored buildings, craft workshops and costumed re-enactments. There's no better place to get a picture of how New York evolved.

A good use for your Metrocard is to take a ride on the Staten Island train, which takes about 40 minutes to travel its none-too-picturesque route from the ferry to Tottenville and includes a great view of the mighty Brooklyn-bound Verrazano-Narrows Bridge.

INFORMATION

✚ Off map at A14
🖻 Staten Island Ferry (➤ 53)

Snug Harbor Cultural Center
✉ 1000 Richmond Terrace
☎ 718/448 2500
🕐 8AM–dusk
🚌 S40
🍴 Melville's Café
♿ Good
💲 Free

Richmondtown
✉ 441 Clarke Avenue
☎ 718/351 1611
🕐 Apr–Dec: Wed–Sun 1–5.
   Jan–Mar: Wed–Fri 1–5
🚌 S74
🍴 Tavern
♿ Good
💲 Inexpensive

Snug Harbor

WHAT'S ON

For more information on events, see also pages 58, 60, 79 and 82.

January/February	*Chinese New Year parades* ✉ Chinatown
March	*St. Patrick's Day Parade* (17 Mar) ✉ Fifth Avenue, 44th–86th Streets
March/April	*Easter Parade* ✉ Fifth Avenue, 44th–59th Streets
April	*Baseball season* (Apr till Oct) ✉ Yankee Stadium, E 161st Street, Bronx ☎ Ticketmaster 212/307 1212; Shea Stadium, Flushing, Queens ☎ 718/507 8499
May	*Ninth Avenue International Food Festival* ✉ Ninth Avenue, 37th–57th Streets ☎ 212/582 7217
	Martin Luther King Day Parade (3rd Sun) ✉ Fifth Avenue, 44th–86th Streets
June	*Metropolitan Opera park concerts* ☎ 212/362 6000
	JVC Jazz Festival: various venues ☎ 212/501 1390
	Lesbian and Gay Pride Parade ☎ 212/463 9030
July 4	*Independence Day* (➤ 82): Stars and Stripes ✉ Regatta South Street, Seaport ☎ 212/669 9400
July–August	*Shakespeare in the Park*: Delacorte Theater ☎ 212/539 8750
	NY Philharmonic park concerts ☎ 212/721 6500
August	*Harlem Week* ☎ 212/427 7200
August–September	*Lincoln Center Out-of-Doors Festival* (➤ 82) ☎ 212/875 5400
	US Open Tennis Championships ☎ 718/760 6200
September	*Feast of San Gennaro*: Little Italy
September–October	*New York Film Festival*: Lincoln Center ☎ 212/875 5050
October	*Blessing of the Animals*: St John the Divine ☎ 212/316 7400
	Columbus Day Parade ✉ Fifth Avenue, 44th–86th Streets
	Halloween Parade: Greenwich Village ☎ 914/758 5519
November	*NYC Marathon*: Verrazano-Narrows Bridge ☎ 212/860 4455
	Macy's Thanksgiving Day Parade ✉ Central Park West around 81st Street ☎ 212/494 5432
December	*Tree Lighting Ceremony*: Rockefeller Center ☎ 212/632 3975
	New Year's Eve: Times Square, ball drops at midnight ☎ 212/768 1560

NEW YORK's
top 25 sights

*The sights are numbered from
south to north through the city*

CONEY ISLAND

INFORMATION

- ✚ Off map at A14
- ✉ Surf Avenue, Boardwalk, Brooklyn. Aquarium: W8th Street, Surf Avenue
- ☎ Aquarium 718/265 3474. Sideshow 718/372 5159
- ◉ Aquarium daily 10–5; summer weekends and holidays 10–7
- 🍴 Cafeteria at Aquarium
- Ⓜ B, D, F Stillwell Avenue/Coney Island, W8th Street, NY Aquarium
- 🚌 B36, B68
- ♿ Good
- Aquarium moderate

Half slummy neighbourhood with the skeleton of a fairground, half sunny seashore playground with a wonderful boardwalk, Coney Island is redolent with other people's memories.

Nathan's and the Cyclone At the end of the last century, Coney Island on a peak day played host to a million people, attracted by Brooklyn's fresh sea air and by Luna Park, Dreamland and Steeplechase Park fairgrounds. By 1921, a boardwalk and the subway had joined the list of attractions, then 1939–40 added the biggest draw of all, the 'Parachute jump'. At the end of this century, that machine is still there, a rusted ghost like a giant spider on stilts, and the glory days of Luna Park are long since gone, yet seedy Coney Island still draws a crowd. The big dipper ride, the Cyclone, is still there, more terrifying for the possibility of collapse than for the thrill of the ride (although it's not at all bad), and Nathan's Famous hot dogs are still sold from the original site, plus candy floss, saltwater taffy (toffee-like confection), and corn dogs (deep fried frankfurters in cornmeal batter).

Fish and fleamarket The New York Aquarium, watery branch of the Bronx Zoo, moved here in 1957. Roughly 10,000 creatures call it home, including beluga whales, coral, a penguin colony and five varieties of shark. It's quite as wonderful as it sounds. The boardwalk Sideshow, though boasting an elastic lady and the blockhead (he hammers nails into his brain), is not such a freak show as it sounds. It's a theatrical performance by East Village arty types.

The boardwalk along Brighton Beach, Coney Island

STATUE OF LIBERTY

Not only does the green lady symbolise the American dream of freedom, but she quite takes your breath away, however many times you've seen her photograph – and despite her surprisingly modest stature.

How she grew In the late 1860s, sculptor Frédéric-Auguste Bartholdi dreamed of placing a monument to freedom in a prominent place. His dream merged with the French historian Edouard-René de Laboulaye's idea of presenting the American people with a statue that celebrated freedom and the two nations' friendship. Part of the idea was to shame the repressive French government, but, apparently, New Yorkers took their freedom for granted, and it was only after Joseph Pulitzer promised to print the name of every donor in his newspaper, the *New York World*, that the city's ordinary citizens coughed up the funds to build the statue's pedestal. She was finally unveiled by President Grover Cleveland on 28 October, 1886, in a ceremony from which women were banned.

Mother of exiles Emma Lazarus's stirring poem, *The New Colossus*, is engraved on the pedestal, while the tablet reads: July IV MDCCLXXVI – the date of the Declaration of Independence. Beneath her size 107 feet, she tramples the broken shackles of tyranny, and her seven-pointed crown beams liberty to the seven continents and the seven seas.

What is she made of? Gustave Eiffel practised for his later work by designing the 1,700-bar iron and steel structure that supports her. She weighs 225 tons, is 151 feet tall, has an 8-foot index finger and a skin of 300 copper plates. The torch tip towers 305 feet above sea level.

HIGHLIGHTS

- Climb to the crown
- View from the pedestal
- Statue of Liberty Museum
- Fort Wood, the star-shaped pedestal base
- Her new centenary flame

INFORMATION

- ✚ Off map at A14
- ✉ Liberty Island
- ☎ 212/363 3200. Ferry 212/269 5755
- ⏱ Jul–Aug: daily 9–6. Sep–Jun: daily 9:30–5. Closed 25 Dec
- 🍴 Cafeteria
- 🚇 1, 9 South Ferry; 4, 5 Bowling Green; N, R Whitehall Street
- 🚌 M1, M6, M15 South Ferry
- ⛴ Ferry departs Battery Park South Ferry (A13). Tickets from Castle Clinton National Monument, Battery Park
- ♿ Poor
- 💲 Inexpensive
- ↔ Battery Park City (▶ 15), Ellis Island (▶ 26), Staten Island Ferry (▶ 53)
- ❓ Audio tours available

3

ELLIS ISLAND

One of the city's newer museums offers the near-compulsory humbling taste of how the huddled masses of new immigrants were not allowed to go free until they'd been herded through these halls, weighed, measured and rubber stamped.

HIGHLIGHTS

- Wall of Honor
- Treasures from Home
- Oral History Studio
- Dormitory
- Augustus Sherman's photos
- View of lower Manhattan

INFORMATION

- ✚ Off map at A14
- ✉ Ellis Island
- ☎ 212/363 3200
- 🕐 Jul–Aug: daily 9–6. Sep–Jun: 9:30–5. Closed 25 Dec
- 🍴 Café
- Ⓢ 1, 9 South Ferry; 4, 5 Bowling Green; N, R Whitehall Street
- 🚌 M1, M6, M15
- 🚢 Ferry departs Battery Park South Ferry (A13). Tickets from Castle Clinton National Monument, Battery Park
- ♿ Good
- 💰 Inexpensive
- ↔ Battery Park City (➤ 15), Statue of Liberty (➤ 25), Staten Island Ferry (➤ 53)
- ❓ Audio tours available

Half of all America It was the poor who docked at Ellis Island after sometimes gruelling voyages in steerage, since first-class passage included permission to decant straight into Manhattan. Annie Moore, aged 15 and the first immigrant to disembark here, arrived in 1892, followed by 16 million founding fathers over the next 40 years, including such then-fledgling Americans as Irving Berlin and Frank Capra. Half the population of the United States can trace their roots to an Ellis Island immigrant.

Island of tears The exhibition in the main building conveys the indignities, frustrations and, above all, fears of the arrivals. (As soon as you arrive, collect your free ticket for the half-hour film, *Island of Hope/Island of Tears*, which you'll otherwise end up missing.) You are guided around more or less the same route the millions took: from the Baggage Room, where they had to abandon all they owned; on to the enormous Registry Room, now bare not only of people, but of furniture too; and on through the series of inspection chambers where medical, mental and political status were ascertained. The Oral History Studio brings it all to life as immigrants recount their experience – especially moving when coupled with the poignant possessions in the Treasures from Home exhibit. All this makes for a demanding few hours' sightseeing, which you'll probably be combining with the Statue of Liberty, since the ferries stop at both islands. Wear sensible shoes and bring lunch.

Top: the Ellis Island National Monument

SOUTH STREET SEAPORT

This reconstructed historic maritime district, with its cobbled streets, is something of a tourist trap. However, when you stroll the boardwalk on a summer's night, with the moon over the East River, you are very glad to be a tourist.

Pier, cruise, shop, eat The seaside/cruise-ship atmosphere is what's fun at the Pier 17 Pavilion,

The Seaport in the evening

which juts 400 feet into the East River, overlooking Brooklyn Heights. It's a mall, with chain stores, bad restaurants and a food court, but also three storeys of charming wooden decks. The adjoining piers, 16 and 15, harbour a number of historic vessels with picturesque arrangements of rigging, plus the replica side-

wheeler, *Andrew Fletcher*, and the 1885 schooner, *Pioneer*, which give harbour cruises. On land, your cash is courted by many shops, housed in the 1812 Federal-style warehouses of Schermerhorn Row – Manhattan's oldest block – and around Water, Front, and Fulton Streets, and also by the few remaining cafés in the old Fulton Market.

Many museums The Seaport Museum Visitors' Center acts as clearing house for all the small-scale exhibitions here. One ticket admits you to: the second-biggest sailing ship ever built, the *Peking*; the floating lighthouse, *Ambrose*; the Children's Center; the Seaport Museum Gallery; a recreation of a 19th-century printer's shop; various walking tours and more.

HIGHLIGHTS

- View of Brooklyn Heights
- Richard Haas' Brooklyn Bridge mural
- Late night forays in the Fulton Fish Market (midnight–8AM)
- Boarding *Andrew Fletcher*
- Watching the Wall Street young decant into the bars around 5PM
- *Titanic* Memorial
- Chandlery
- Fulton Market (especially the bakeries)
- Incongruous giant bubble (tennis courts!)
- The sea breeze

INFORMATION

- ✚ B12–B13
- ✉ Visitor Center: 12 Fulton Street. Tickets also from Pier 16
- ☎ 212/669 9424
- 🕐 Jun–Sep: Fri–Wed 10–6. Oct–May: Fri–Wed 10–5. Closed Dec 25 and Jan 1
- 🍴 Numerous
- 🚇 2, 3, 4, 5, J, M, Z Fulton Street; A, C Broadway/Nassau Street
- 🚌 M15 Pearl/Fulton Street
- ♿ Poor
- 💲 Inexpensive
- ↔ World Trade Center (▶ 28), Brooklyn Bridge (▶ 29)
- ❓ Walking tours: 'Ship Restoration', 'Back Streets'

WORLD TRADE CENTER

Not much liked when they went up (and up and up) in the 1970s, the 'twin towers' practically define the lower Manhattan skyline. Four boring buildings, a hotel and a mall complete the centre, but the view is the point.

Scary skyscrapers The twin towers are like jellyfish in that their outer covering is all that holds them together. Minoru Yamasaki's design replaced the steel skeleton of the average skyscraper with load-bearing exterior walls of vertical columns and gigantic horizontal spandrel beams. Large windows for the workers' warren inside were sacrificed. In February 1993, the foundations were very nearly rocked by a bomb left in the underground car park.

Vital statistics The towers' 110 floors rise 1,350 feet, or a quarter of a mile, supplying 10 million square feet of office space for 50,000 workers. Each tower contains 99 lifts, but the 80,000 daily visitors are allocated a single express that reaches the 107th floor of Tower Two in 58 seconds flat. Over 1,000 people were injured in the 1993 bomb blast, and over $2 million worth of wine was blasted from the bottles of the restaurant, Cellar in the Sky, now replaced by Windows on the World.

No vertigo After they were finished in 1973, the towers attracted aerial mayhem. Philippe Petit walked a towertop-to-towertop tightrope in August 1974, for which he was arrested and ordered to do kids' shows in Central Park. A year later, Owen Quinn parachuted off. Recklessness charges were dropped. Finally, in May 1977, George Willig, using crampons of his own design, climbed up a tower. The city sued for a quarter of a million, but accepted $1.10.

BROOKLYN BRIDGE

The view from the bridge is spectacular, but the structure itself, with its twin Gothic towers and ballet of cables, means the first Manhattan–Brooklyn link fulfils beautifully its symbolic role of affording entry into new worlds of opportunity.

Killer bridge In 1869, before construction had even started, the original engineer, John Roebling, had his foot crushed by a ferry and died of gangrene three weeks later. His son, Washington, took over the project, only to succumb to the bends and subsequent paralysis. Washington's wife, Emily Warren, finished overseeing the construction, during which 20 workmen died in various nasty accidents. Then, on 30 May, 1883, a few days after the opening, a woman fell over, screamed, and set off a 20,000-person stampede, which claimed 12 more lives. Robert Odlum's was the first non-accidental bridge-related death. He jumped off for a bet in 1885 and died from internal bleeding later.

Bridge of sighs Now, the occasional leaper chooses the cable walk as his or her last, but things are mostly peaceful. The best time and direction to walk the renovated (in 1983) footpath is east from Brooklyn to Manhattan at dusk. The sun sets behind Liberty Island and, as you stroll on, down-town looms larger and larger, the sky darkens to cobalt, the lights go on, the skyline goes sparkly, and you are swallowed into the metropolis. It's a transcendental half-hour. Although you'll almost certainly be fine, it's still not a good idea to walk the bridge at night, especially carrying cameras. And keep to the uptown side; the other lane is for bikes.

HIGHLIGHTS

- Walk to Manhattan
- Panorama of NY buildings
- Cables – each of 5,282 wires
- Jehovah's Witnesses' *Watchtower* HQ
- Cars hurtling, 6 yards below your feet
- Cyclists hurtling, 6 inches from your face

INFORMATION

- ✚ C13
- ✉ Walkway entrance is across Park Row from City Hall Park
- 🚇 4, 5, 6 Brooklyn Bridge/City Hall; J, M, Z Chambers Street
- 🚌 M1, M6
- ♿ Good
- ✋ Free
- 🔄 South Street Seaport (➤ 27)

The Lower Manhattan skyline from beneath Brooklyn Bridge

CHINATOWN

HIGHLIGHTS

- Buddhist temple (✉ 64B Mott Street)
- Chinatown History Museum (✉ 70 Mulberry Street)
- Pearl River Mart (✉ 277 Canal Street)
- Doyers Street: once the 'Bloody Angle'
- Chinatown Ice Cream Factory (✉ 65 Bayard Street)
- Columbus Park (✉ Bayard/Baxter Streets)
- The Tombs, or Criminal Courts Building (✉ 100 Centre Street)
- Cecilia Tam's egg cakes (✉ Mosco/Mott Streets)

INFORMATION

- ✚ C11–C12
- ✉ Roughly delineated by Worth Street/East Broadway, the Bowery, Grand Street, Centre Street
- ◉ Some restaurants close around 10PM
- 🍴 Numerous
- Ⓡ J, M, Z, N, R, 6, A, C, E, 1, 9 Canal Street; B, D Grand Street
- 🚍 M1, B51
- ♿ Poor
- ↔ Little Italy (▶ 54), Lower East Side Tenement Museum (▶ 55)
- ❓ General tours ☎ 212/619 4785. Chinese herbal medicine tours ☎ 212/219 2527

New York's Chinatown, the largest in the West, encroaches on what remains of Little Italy and the Jewish Lower East Side, even on Hispanic 'Loisaida', Wander here, and you're humbled by the sight of a lifestyle that, making no concessions to the visitor, continues to thrive.

Going west Prefiguring the movement of immigrants from the devolved Russia and Eastern Europe of today, Chinese people first came to New York in the late 19th century, looking to work a while, make some money and return home. But, by 1880 or so, some 10,000 men – mostly Cantonese railroad workers decamped from California – had been stranded between Canal, Worth and Baxter Streets. Tongs (sort of secret mafia operations) were formed, and still keep order today over some 150,000 Chinese, Taiwanese, Vietnamese, Burmese and Singaporeans. New York, incidentally, has two more Chinatowns: in Flushing, Queens, and Eighth Avenue, Brooklyn, with a further 150,000-odd inhabitants.

A closed world Although you may happily wander its colourful, slightly manic, streets, you will never penetrate Chinatown. Many of its denizens never learn English, never leave its environs, and never wish to. The 600 factories and 350 restaurants keep them in work; then there are the tea shops, mah-jong parlours, herbalists, fishmongers and the highest bank-to-citizen ratio in New York, in which Chinese stash their wages (normally not more than $10–$20,000 a year) to save for the 'eight bigs' (car, television, video recorder, fridge, camera, phone, washing machine and furniture), to send home, or eventually to invest in a business of their own.

GREENWICH VILLAGE

This sugar-sweet picturesque, human-scale neighbourhood of brownstones and actual trees is the other romantic image of Manhattan (second to the skyline), familiar from sitcoms and films. Its dense streets are rewarding to wander.

What village? It was named after Greenwich, south-east London, by the British colonists who settled here at the end of the 17th century. In the 18th and early 19th centuries the wealthy founders of New York society took refuge here from smallpox, cholera and yellow fever.

Bohemia, academe, jazz When the élite moved on and up, the bohemian invasion began, pioneered by Edgar Allan Poe, who moved to 85 W 3rd Street in 1845. Fellow literary habitués included: Mark Twain, O Henry, Walt Whitman, F Scott Fitzgerald, Eugene O'Neill, John Dos Passos and e e cummings. New York University arrived in Washington Square in 1831 and grew into the country's largest private university. Post World War II, bohemia became beatnik; a group of abstract artists, centred around Jackson Pollock, Mark Rothko and Willem de Kooning, also found a home here.

Freedom parades Café Society, where Billie Holiday made her 1938 debut, was one of the first non-racially segregated clubs in New York. Thirty years later, a different kind of discrimination was challenged, when police raided the Stonewall Inn on 28 June, 1969, arresting gay men for illegally buying drinks and setting off the Stonewall Riots—the birth of the Gay Rights movement. The Inn stood on Christopher Street, which became the main drag (no pun intended) of New York's gay community, and ranked with San Francisco for excitement.

HIGHLIGHTS

- Cafés
- Jazz clubs
- Washington Square Park
- NYC's narrowest house (✉ 75 Bedford Street)
- West (of Hudson Street) Village
- Halloween Parade
- Jefferson Market Library
- Balducci's (the grocers)
- Minetta Lane
- Carmine Street pool (Clarkson Avenue/Seventh Avenue South)

Washington Memorial Arch

INFORMATION

- ✚ B9–C9
- ✉ East to west from Broadway to Hudson Street; north to south from 14th Street to Houston Street
- 🍴 Numerous
- 🚇 A, C, E, B, D, F W4th Street; 1, 9 Christopher Street
- 🚌 M10
- 🚆 PATH Christopher Street
- ♿ Poor
- ↔ SoHo (► 54)

31

UNION SQUARE

INFORMATION

- D9
- W14th–17th Streets, Park Avenue South, Broadway
- Greenmarket 212/ 788 7900
- Greenmarket Mon, Wed, Fri, Sat 8–6
- Numerous
- 4, 5, 6, L, N, R 14th Street, Union Square
- M3
- Poor

For proof that New York evolves constantly, see Union Square. A 'needle park' in the 1970s, it's now where downtown and up meet, with great restaurants, a wild café scene and the egalitarian highlight of all Manhattan: the Greenmarket.

Not those Unions Laid out in 1839, Union Square had close encounters with socialism though its name actually refers to the union of Broadway and Fourth Avenue. It was a mecca for soapbox orators in the first three decades of this century, then, during the 1930 Depression, 35,000 unemployed rallied here en route to City Hall to demand work; workers' May Day celebrations convened here too. Later, Andy Warhol picked up the vibes, set up his factory (on the south-west corner), and began publishing his style mag, *Interview*, where once the *Daily Worker* had been produced.

Green In summer, the park teems with office refugees, sharing the lawn with an equestrian George Washington by John Quincy Adams Ward, an Abe Lincoln by Henry Kirke Brown, and a Marquis de Lafayette, which Frédéric-Auguste Bartholdi (of subsequent Statue of Liberty fame) gave the city in 1876. Mondays, Wednesdays, Fridays and Saturdays are Greenmarket days. An entire culture, an actual Manhattan lifestyle, has grown around this collation of stalls overflowing with home-grown and home-made produce from New England farmers, fishers, bakers and growers. Everyone has their favourite farmer. Cult highlights include: the maple candies, the Amish cheeses, the Pretzel Man (and his pretzels), the fresh clams, the sugarfree muffins and the hundred blends of mesclun salad. Curiously, the square also harbours some of the city's tackiest superstores.

EMPIRE STATE BUILDING

It was not Fay Wray's fault, nor Cary Grant's in An Affair to Remember, *that this is the most famous skyscraper in the world. Rather, its fame is the reason that it has appeared in every New York movie. You have to climb this.*

King for 40 years This is the very definition of 'skyscraper', and it was the highest man-made thing until the World Trade Center went up in the 1970s. Construction began in 1929, not long before the great Wall Street Crash, and by the time it was topped in 1931 – construction went at the superfast rate of four storeys a week – so few could afford to rent space, they called it 'the Empty State Building'. Only the popularity of its observatories kept the wolves from the door. These viewpoints still attract around 35,000 visitors a day. Many stop off on the Mezzanine for the newest attraction, the New York Skyride, which simulates a rooftop flight, including a hair-raising virtual crash over Wall Street; the tour guide is James Doohan – *Star Trek*'s 'Scottie'.

The numbers It is 1,250 feet high, and there are 102 floors. The frame contains 60,000 tons of steel, 10 million bricks line the building and there are 6,500 windows taking up five acres. The speediest of the 73 lifts climb 1,200 feet per minute. The speediest runners in the annual Empire State Run-Up climb almost 170 steps per minute, making the 1,860 steps to the 102nd floor in 11 minutes – though normal people take about half an hour to climb down! It is not necessarily worth the (up to 60-minute) wait to climb the extra 16 floors to the glass-encased 102nd floor.

HIGHLIGHTS

- The view: by day, at dusk, and by night
- The view up from 34th Street
- New York Skyride
- Penny-flattening machine
- Lights on the top 30 storeys (4th July, Halloween and Christmas)

INFORMATION

- ✚ D7
- ✉ 350 Fifth Avenue (W34th Street)
- ☎ 212/736 3100
- 🕐 Daily 9:30AM–midnight (last admission 11:30PM)
- 🍴 Snack bar
- Ⓜ B, D, F, N, R 34th Street
- 🚌 M1, M2, M3, M4, M5, M16, M34
- 🚇 PATH 33rd Street
- ♿ Good
- 💲 Inexpensive
- ↔ NY Public Library (➤ 34), Chrysler Building (➤ 35), Macy's (➤ 71)

Top: the view
Below: the entrance hall

11

NEW YORK PUBLIC LIBRARY

HIGHLIGHTS

- Patience and Fortitude
- 'Truth' and 'Beauty'
- T S Eliot's typed *The Waste Land*
- Jefferson's handwritten Declaration of Independence
- Astor Hall
- The shop
- Thomas Hastings' flagpost bases
- Gottesman Hall ceiling

INFORMATION

- ✚ D6
- ✉ 476 Fifth Avenue (42nd Street)
- ☎ 212/869 8089
- ◷ Thu–Sat 10–6; Tue–Wed 11–7:30. Closed holidays
- 🍴 Kiosks outside (not winter)
- Ⓜ 4, 5, 6, 7, S 42nd Street Grand Central
- 🚌 M101, M102
- 🚆 Metro North, Grand Central
- ♿ Good (also see below)
- 💲 Free
- ↔ Empire State Building (► 33), Chrysler Building (► 35), Grand Central Terminal (► 36), Bryant Park (► 58)
- ❓ Tours 11AM and 2PM daily. Notable branches include the Andrew Heiskell Library for the Blind and Physically Handicapped (✉ 40 W 20th Street) and the Library for the Performing Arts (✉ 40 Lincoln Plaza)

Why are we sending you to a library on your holidays? Because the New York Public Library's Central Research Building is a great, white, hushed palace, beautiful to behold even if you have no time to open a book.

The building Carrère and Hastings (who also designed the Frick, ► 41) were the architects responsible for what is generally thought the city's best representative of the *beaux-arts* style – the sumptuous yet classical French school that flourished in New York's 'gilded age', about 1880–1920. A pair of lions, which Mayor La Guardia christened Patience and Fortitude, flank the majestic stairway that leads directly into the barrel-vaulted, carved white marble temple of Astor Hall. The lions are themselves flanked by fountains, 'Truth' and 'Beauty', which echo the site's previous (1845–99) incarnation as the Croton Reservoir supplying the city's water. Behind this briefly stood New York's version of London's Crystal Palace, built for the first American World's Fair in 1853. Like the London one, it burned down. Inside, see temporary exhibitions in the Gottesman Hall, and look up! The carved oak ceiling is sublime; read in the two-block-long Main Reading Room; see library collection rarities in the Salomon Room; and don't miss the Richard Haas murals of NYC publishing houses in the De Witt Wallace Periodical Room.

The books The library owns over 15 million books, most living in the 82 branches. This building is dedicated to research. The CATNYP computer, complete with dumb waiter, can disgorge any of the 16 million manuscripts or 3 million books from the 92 miles of stacks in ten minutes flat.

CHRYSLER BUILDING

'Which is your favourite New York building?' goes the annoying yet perennial question. As it turns out, nine out of ten people who express a preference choose the Chrysler Building over all others. This should surprise nobody who gazes on it.

King for a year The tower, commissioned from William Van Alen by Walter Chrysler (who asked for something 'taller than the Eiffel Tower'), won the world's tallest building competition in 1930 ... until the Empire State Building went up the following year. Van Alen had been almost beaten by Craig Severance's Bank of Manhattan tower at 40 Wall Street, when his rival, aware of the unofficial race, slung on an extra two feet. Unbeknownst to Severance, though, Van Alen was secretly constructing a 123-foot stainless steel spire, which he 'slotted' out through the 925-foot roof, beating the 927-footer hands down. It is sort of ironic that the best view of the art deco beauty's top is now gained from the observatory at the Empire State.

Multi-storey car Every detail of the 77-storey building evokes the motor car – a 1929 Chrysler Plymouth, to be exact. The winged steel gargoyles are modelled on its radiator caps; other of the building's stepped setbacks carry stylized hub-caps, and the entire spire resembles a radiator grille; and this ain't no Toyota. The golden age of cars is further evoked by the stunning lobby, which you can visit – ostensibly to view the Con Edison (New York's utilities company) conservation exhibit, but really to see the red marble, granite and chrome interior, surmounted by the 97- by 100-foot mural depicting industrial scenes and celebrating 'transport'.

HIGHLIGHTS

- Spire
- Ceiling mural
- Elevator cabs
- Fourth setback gargoyles
- African marble lobby

INFORMATION

- ✚ E6
- ✉ 405 Lexington Avenue (42nd Street)
- 🕐 Mon–Fri 7AM–6PM. Closed holidays
- 🚇 4, 5, 6, 7, S 42nd Street, Grand Central
- 🚌 M101, M102
- 🚆 Metro North, Grand Central
- ♿ Good
- 🎫 Free
- ↔ Empire State Building (➤ 33)

The pinnacle of success

13

GRAND CENTRAL TERMINAL

HIGHLIGHTS

- Main Concourse ceiling
- Oyster Bar
- All the new restaurants
- Mercury on the 42nd Street façade
- The clock
- Free art installations
- The 75-foot arched windows
- Grand Staircase
- Uneven Tennessee marble floor
- Municipal Arts Society tours

INFORMATION

- ✚ E6
- ✉ Park Avenue (42nd Street)
- ☎ 212/532 4900
- ◷ Daily 5:30AM–1:30AM
- 🍴 Restaurant, café/bar, snack bars
- Ⓢ 4, 5, 6, 7, S 42nd Street, Grand Central
- 🚍 M101, 102 Grand Central
- 🚃 Metro North, Grand Central
- ♿ Good
- 🎟 Free
- ↔ Empire State Building (►33), NY Public Library (►34), Chrysler Building (►35), Bryant Park (►58)
- ❓ Tours Wed 12:30PM. Meet by Chemical Bank in Main Concourse

Don't call it a station. All tracks terminate here, which makes this railway mecca a far grander entity. The beaux-arts building bustles like no place else. As the saying goes – stand here long enough, and the entire world passes by.

Heart of the nation 'Grand Central Station!' bellowed (erroneously) the 1937 opening of the eponymous NBC radio drama; "Beneath the glitter and swank of Park Avenue... Crossroads of a million private lives!... Heart of the nation's greatest city...'. And so it is, and has been since 1871 when the first, undersized version was opened by Commodore Cornelius Vanderbilt, who had bought up all the city's railways, just like on a giant Monopoly board. See him in bronze below Jules-Alexis Coutans' allegorical statuary on the main (south, 42nd Street) façade. The current building dates from 1913 and is another *beaux-arts* glory, its design modelled partly on the Paris Opéra by architects Warren and Wetmore. William Wilgus was the logician responsible for traffic-marshalling, while Reed & Stem were the overall engineers. Look up at the main concourse ceiling for the stunning sight of 2,500 'stars' in a cerulean sky, with medieval-style zodiac signs by French artist Paul Helleu.

Meeting under the clock The fame of the four-faced clock atop the information booth is out of all proportion to its size. (You may remember the scene in the film *The Fisher King* where thousands of commuters fell into synchronized waltzing around it.) Beneath the clock, and the ground, is a warren of 32 miles of tracks, tunnels and vaulted chambers, in one the famed Oyster Bar resides. Be careful what you say here – the acoustics are amazing.

ROCKEFELLER CENTER

This small village of famous art deco buildings provides many of those 'Gee, this is New York' moments: especially in winter when you see ice-skaters ringed by the flags of the UN, and gaze up at the massive tree.

Prometheus is here The buildings' bible, Willensky and White's *AIA Guide to NYC*, calls the 19-building Rockefeller Center 'The greatest urban complex of the 20th century'. It is 'the heart of New York', agreed the Landmarks Commission in 1985. So the architectural importance of the centre – and especially the elongated ziggurat GE Building (better known as the RCA Building) – is beyond dispute, but it's still easy to enjoy the place. Rest on a Channel Gardens bench, enjoy the seasonal foliage, and gaze on the lower plaza, the rink and Paul Manship's *Prometheus*. The Channel is a reference to the English Channel, since these sloping gardens separate La Maison Française from the British Empire Building.

Rockefeller the Younger The realisation of John D Rockefeller Jr.'s grand scheme to outdo dad (Mister Standard Oil) provided work for a quarter of a million souls during the Depression. In 1957, Marilyn Monroe detonated the dynamite for the Time & Life building's foundations, and the Center was still growing into the 1970s.

Conan and Rockettes For many years, the NBC Studios in the GE Building hosted the hip TV talk show *Late Night* with David Letterman. Dave decamped to CBS, and the now-famous Conan O'Brian was plucked from obscurity to host the spot. Over on Avenue of the Americas is Radio City Music Hall, landmark home to the Rockettes, born in 1934 and still kicking.

Atlas, *Lee Lawrie*

HIGHLIGHTS

- GE Building, outside
- GE Building's lobbies
- NBC Studio tour
- Skating in winter
- Sea Grill restaurant
- Radio City Music Hall
- Channel Gardens
- *Prometheus*
- Atlas (Fifth Avenue, 50th–51st Street)

INFORMATION

- ✚ E5
- ✉ Fifth–Seventh Avenues (47th–52nd Streets)
- ◉ Various
- 🍴 Numerous restaurants, cafés
- Ⓜ B, D, F 47th–50th Streets, Rockefeller Center
- ▭ M1, M2, M3, M4, M5, M18
- ♿ Moderate
- 🎫 Free
- ↔ MoMA (➤ 38)
- ❓ Radio City tours
  ☎ 212/632 4041.
  NBC Studio tours
  ☎ 212/664 4000

15

MUSEUM OF MODERN ART

INFORMATION

- E5
- 11 W53rd Street
- 212/708 7500
- Fri–Tue 11–6; Thu 11–9. Closed 25 Dec
- Restaurant
- B, D, E Seventh Avenue; E, F Fifth Avenue
- M5, M6, M7, M18
- Few
- Inexpensive

MoMA's modern façade

A great collection housed in a cool building – literally in summer. The film programme is practically the final fling of repertory cinema in New York; even the shop and the popular restaurant are modern and arty.

Van Gogh to Man Ray Founded on the 1931 bequest of Lillie P Bliss, which consisted of 235 works, the MoMA collections now amount to about 100,000 pieces of art. True to the museum's title, these include modern arts: photography, graphic design, household objects, conceptual art and industrial design, though work from the first half of the century is better represented than the really new – go to the Whitney for that. There are four floors, plus the Abby Aldrich Rockefeller Sculpture Garden – where you can retreat from the city in the company of Rodin, Picasso and Moore. The works are arranged more or less chronologically, with temporary shows sharing the upper floors with architecture and design.

Post-Impressionists to Graffiti artists The collection starts in the late 19th century, with the Post-Impressionists and Fauvists: Cézanne, Van Gogh, Monet, Manet, Pissarro, Seurat, Gauguin and Matisse. Most movements of this century follow Cubism, Expressionism, Futurism, Surrealism and Abstract Expressionism – up to and including Pop (Oldenburg, Dine, Rauschenberg, and Warhol, of course) – and the 'Graffiti' work of Keith Haring and Jean-Michel Basquiat. What was probably MoMA's most famous and important painting of all no longer hangs here. It was Picasso's 1937 *Guernica*, which, post-Franco, was given back to the Spanish.

LINCOLN CENTER

Strolling to the fantastically fairy-lit ten-storey Metropolitan Opera House colonnade across the Central Plaza on a winter's night is one of the most glamorous things you can do on this earth, and you don't need tickets.

West Side Story The ambitious Rockefeller-funded über-arts centre was envisaged in the late 1950s and finished in 1969, after 7,000 families and 800 businesses had been kicked out of their homes by developer Robert Moses and the John D Rockefeller millions. Much of *West Side Story* was actually shot on these streets after the demolition had begun, capturing the pain of change forever.

All the arts The 15 acres include megahouses for the biggest-scale arts, all designed by different architects in the same white travertine. The Metropolitan Opera House is the glamour queen, with her vast Marc Chagall murals, miles of red carpet, swooshes of stair and starry chandeliers that swiftly, silently and thrillingly rise to the sky-high gold-leafed ceiling before performances. Avery Fisher Hall caught America's oldest orchestra, the NY Philharmonic, on its trajectory out of Carnegie Hall, while the Juilliard School of Music keeps it supplied with fresh maestri. The New York State Theater, housing the New York City Opera and the New York City Ballet, faces Avery Fisher across the Plaza. Two smaller theatres, the Vivian Beaumont and Mitzi Newhouse, and a more intimate concert hall, Alice Tully, plus the Walter Reade cinema, the little Bruno Walter Auditorium, and the Guggenheim Bandshell for outdoor summer concerts, complete the pack. Over 13,500 arts fans can be swallowed simultaneously. Just don't expect to find a cab afterward.

HIGHLIGHTS

- Chandeliers in the Met auditorium
- Reflecting Pool with Henry Moore's *Reclining Figure*
- Lincoln Center Out-of-Doors Festival
- NY City Ballet's *Nutcracker*
- Chagall murals, Met foyer
- Thursday morning rehearsals, Avery Fisher
- New York Film Festival
- Philip Johnson's Plaza fountain
- Chamber Music Society, Alice Tully
- Annual *Messiah* singalong

INFORMATION

- ✚ D3–D4
- ✉ Broadway (62nd–67th Streets)
- ☎ 212/875 5400. Met 212/362 6000. Avery Fisher 212/875 5030
- 🎭 Enquire for performance times
- 🍴 Restaurants, cafés, bars
- 🚇 1, 9 66th Street Lincoln Center
- 🚌 M5, M7, M104, crosstown M66
- ♿ Good; for information ☎ 212/875 5350
- 💲 Admission to Center free
- ↔ Central Park (▶ 40)
- ❓ Tours leave from concourse under Met, daily 10–5 ☎ 212/875 5350

17

CENTRAL PARK

INFORMATION

- E4–G1
- 212/794 6564 or 800/834 3832. Events 212/360 3456. Loeb Boathouse 212/861 4137. Wildlife Conservation Center 212/861 6030. Swedish Cottage 212/988 9093. Wollman Rink 212/517 4800. Lasker Pool 212/534 7639
- Dairy Information Center Tue–Thu, Sat, Sun 11–5; Fri 1–5
- Restaurants, kiosks
- B, D, A, C Columbus Circle; 72, 81 96th Street; N, R 57th Street; B, Q 57th Street; 4, 5, 6 86th Street; 2, 3 110th Street
- M1, M2, M3, M4, M5, M10, M18. Crosstown M66, M30, M72, M86
- Moderate
- Free
- American Museum of Natural History (➤ 43)

The park is the escape valve on the pressure cooker. Without it New York would explode – especially in summer, when the humidity tops 90 per cent, and bikers, runners, bladers, dog strollers, and frisbee players convene. It's a way of life.

Olmsted, Vaux and the Greensward Plan In the middle of the last century, when there was no Manhattan north of 42nd Street, *New York Evening Post* editor, William Cullen Bryant, campaigned until the city invested the fortune of $5m in an 840-acre wasteland swarming with pig-farming squatters who ran bone-boiling operations. Responsible for clearing the land was journalist Frederick Law Olmsted, who, with English architect Calvert Vaux, also won the competition to design the park, with his 'Greensward Plan'. By day, Olmsted supervised the shifting of 5 million cubic tons of dirt; by night, he and Vaux trod the wasteland acres and designed. Night strolls are not recommended nowadays.

Fun and games Start at the Dairy Information Center, and pick up a map and events list. These show the lie of the land and tell you about the Wildlife Conservation Center (Zoo), the Carousel, the playgrounds, rinks, fountains, statues and Strawberry Fields, where John Lennon is commemorated close to the Dakota Building where he lived and was shot. But the busy life of the park is not recorded on maps: showing off rollerblade moves on the Mall by the Sheep Meadow; hanging out at the Heckscher Playground and Great Lawn softball leagues; doing the loop road fast, by bike; sunbathing, poolside, at the vast Lasker Pool in Harlem; playing rowboat dodgems on the Lake; bouldering on the outcrops of Manhattan schist...

FRICK COLLECTION

Like the Wallace Collection in London and the Musée Picasso in Paris, Henry Clay Frick's mansion is half the reason for seeing his collection. Henry bequeathed these riches to the nation as a memorial to himself – that's the kind of guy he was.

The mansion, and the man Henry Clay Frick was chairman of the Carnegie Steel Corp (US Steel). He was one of the most ruthless strike-breakers of all time and the nastiest industrialist of his day. Instead of any come-uppance (though there were several assassination attempts), he got to commission Carrère and Hastings (who designed the NY Public Library) to build him one of the last great *beaux-arts* mansions on Fifth Avenue and fill it with an exquisite collection of 14th- to 19th-century old masters, porcelain, furniture and bronzes. Not much of the furniture is velvet-roped, so you can rest your limbs in a Louis XVI chair before taking a stroll in the central glass-roofed courtyard and the gorgeous garden.

What Frick bought Certain rooms of the 40-room mansion are arranged around a particular work or artist, notably the Boucher Room, just east of the entrance, and especially the Fragonard Room, with the 11-painting *Progress of Love* series. There are British masters (Constable, Whistler, Turner, Gainsborough), Dutch (Vermeer, Rembrandt, Van Eyck, Hals), Italian (Titian, Bellini, Veronese), and Spanish (El Greco, Velázquez, Goya). Interspersed are Limoges enamel and Chinese porcelain, Persian carpets and Marie Antoinette's furniture. Some Frick descendants still have keys to this modest *pied à terre*, which, as well as what you see, has a bowling alley in the basement.

HIGHLIGHTS

- *The Progress of Love,* Fragonard
- *Mall in St James's Park,* Gainsborough
- *Sir Thomas More,* Holbein
- *Officer and the Laughing Girl,* Vermeer
- *The Polish Rider,* Rembrandt
- *Virgin and Child with Saints,* Van Eyck
- *Lady Meux,* Whistler
- *Philip IV of Spain,* Velázquez
- *The Russell Page garden*

INFORMATION

- ✚ F4
- ✉ 1 E70th Street
- ☎ 212/288 0700
- 🕐 Tue–Sat 10–6; Sun 1–6. Closed holidays
- 🍴 None
- 🚇 6 68th Street
- 🚌 M1, M2, M3, M4
- ♿ Good
- 💲 Inexpensive
- ↔ Central Park (➤ 40)
- ❓ Lectures: Wed 5:30

Virgin and Child with Saints, *Van Eyck*

19

WHITNEY MUSEUM OF AMERICAN ART

HIGHLIGHTS

- Biennial
- *Circus*, Alexander Calder
- The Hoppers
- The O'Keeffes
- *Dempsey and Firpo*, George Bellows
- The Louise Nevelsons
- Drawbridge

INFORMATION

- ✚ F3
- ✉ 945 Madison Avenue
- ☎ 212/570 3600
- ⊙ Wed, Fri–Sun 11–6; Thu 1–8. Closed holidays
- 🍴 Café
- Ⓢ 6 77th Street
- ⊟ M1, M2, M3, M4
- ♿ Good
- 🅿 Inexpensive
- ❓ Lectures, video/film: Whitney at the Philip Morris Building ✉ Park Avenue (42nd Street) ☎ 212/878 2550 ⊙ Mon–Fri 11–6. Closed holidays

More modern than the Modern, the Whitney wants to be as unpredictable as the artist du jour, and very often succeeds. It's a New York tradition to sneer at the Biennial, whether or not one has seen the show.

No room at the Met Sculptor and patron of her contemporaries' work, Gertrude Vanderbilt Whitney offered her collection to the Met in 1929, but the great institution turned up its nose, and Whitney was forced to found the Whitney. In 1966, Marcel Breuer's cantilevered, granite-clad, Brutalist block was completed to house it in suitably controversial manner, and here it lours still, not universally loved, but impossible to overlook. The Whitney's core collection now reads like a roll-call of the American (and immigrant) greats from earlier this century: Edward Hopper, Thomas Hart Benton, Willem de Kooning, Georgia O'Keeffe, Claes Oldenburg, Jasper Johns, George Bellows, Jackson Pollock are a few (the male to female ratio has improved, but barely). Let's hope the curators and buyers are as good as Gertrude at spotting talent for the future. There are so many more artists these days …

Take your pick From the important and delicious collections, work often emphasises a single artist's work, other times proving more eclectic. There's an active film and video department and two branches. There used to be four branches in Manhattan alone during the art boomtime of the 1980s. The Whitney Biennial (in the spring of odd-numbered years) provides an echo of those days, when the New York art pack gets sweaty debating the merits and demerits of the chosen few on show and of the curator's vision – for the Biennial is invitational, and makes careers.

AMERICAN MUSEUM OF NATURAL HISTORY

No longer a lovable anachronism since extensive renovations, this 125-year-old hulk is stuffed with dinosaur skeletons to pacify bawling brats, but the best things are the blue whale's cocktail bar and the low-tech dioramas.

Who's who Of the 36 million things owned by the museum – which is, needless to say, the largest such institution in the world – only a small percentage is on show. Among the improvements implemented by the $45-million cash injection has been a sprucing-up of the buildings themselves, cleaning up windows and revealing original features. The fourth floor (where all vertebrate fossils, including dinosaurs, are found) now comes complete with partially interactive dinosaurs to please computer-jaded children. There's far too much to see in one day, with three city blocks and the entire evolution of life on earth covered. Not-to-be-missed items include the barosaurus rearing up to her full 55 feet to protect her young from a T-rex attack; and, on the first floor, the 94-foot blue whale which dominates the two-storey Hall of Ocean Life and Biology of Fishes and presides over its own bar.

More gems Another highlight is the 563-carat Star of India blue star sapphire, part of the unbelievable Hall of Meteorites, Minerals and Gems, containing almost $50-million worth of precious stones, plus the 34-ton Ahnighito meteorite. The cutest part of the museum is where animals of all sizes are displayed behind glass in *tableaux vivants* of considerable artistic merit. Adjoining sub-museums include the astronomy department's Hayden Planetarium, containing the Guggenheim Space Theater and the Sky Theater; and the Nature Max theatre, where a four-storey screen shows ecological blockbusters.

HIGHLIGHTS

- Blue whale
- Barosaurus
- Herd of stuffed elephants
- New dinosaur halls
- Hall of Human Biology and Evolution
- Sky Shows
- Star of India
- The dioramas
- Dinosaur embryo
- The 'Diner Saurus' (fast food)

INFORMATION

- ✚ E2
- ✉ Central Park West (79th Street)
- ☎ 212/769 5100
- 🕐 Mon–Thu, Sun 10–5:45; Fri–Sat 10–8:45
- 🍴 Various
- Ⓑ B, C 81st Street
- 🚌 M7, M10, M11, M79
- ♿ Good
- 💲 Moderate
- ↔ Lincoln Center (► 39), Central Park (► 40)
- ❓ 75min tours until 3:15. Hayden Planetarium ☎ 212/769 5920

The barosaurus

21

METROPOLITAN MUSEUM OF ART

HIGHLIGHTS

- Temple of Dendur
- Period rooms, American Wing
- *Diptych*, Van Eyck
- *Young Woman with a Water Jug*, Vermeer
- *Venus and Adonis*, Rubens
- *Grand Canal, Venice*, Turner
- *Sunflowers*, Van Gogh
- *Madame X*, Sargent
- Rooftop Sculpture Garden

The Great Hall

INFORMATION

- F3
- 1000 Fifth Avenue (82nd Street)
- 212/535 7710
- Tue, Wed, Sun 9:30–5:15; Fri, Sat 9:30–8.45. Closed 25 Dec, 1 Jan
- Cafeteria, restaurant, bar
- 4, 5, 6 86th Street
- M1, M2, M3, M4
- Good
- Inexpensive
- Central Park (► 40), Whitney (► 42), Guggenheim (► 45)
- The Cloisters (► 48) houses more of the Met's medieval collections. Same-day admission on Met ticket

It will give you bigger blisters than the Uffizi, bigger chills than the Sistine Chapel, and take a bigger slice of holiday time than all dinners. It's so big, it doesn't just contain Egyptian artefacts, but an entire Egyptian building.

Art city The limestone *beaux-arts* façade with its tremendous steps was a 1902 addition to the Calvert Vaux (of Central Park fame) red-brick Gothic building buried inside here. There are several more buildings-within-buildings, interior gardens and courtyards, such is the scale of the Met. The 15 BC Temple of Dendur, in its glass-walled bemoated chamber east of the main entrance on the first floor, is the best known, but there's much more besides: the Astor Court above it – a replica Ming dynasty scholar's court-yard – plus, in the American Wing, a score of period-style rooms, and the vast and sunlit garden court with its hodgepodge of Tiffany glass and topiary, a Frank Lloyd Wright window and the entire Federal-style façade of the United States Bank from Wall Street.

Where to start? How to stop? A quarter of the 3 million-plus objects are up at any one time, so pace yourself. Relax. There are about 15 discrete collections. Some visitors decide on one or two per visit – 13th- to 18th-century European Paintings (or part thereof) and Ancient Art, perhaps – and leave it at that. Or you could structure a route around one or two favourite and familiar works. The Information Center on the ground floor Uris Center, with its Orientation Theater and giant floor plans, is the place to begin, whatever you decide to see. Consider visiting on Friday or Saturday evening, when a string quartet serenades you, and there are far fewer crowds.

SOLOMON R GUGGENHEIM MUSEUM

If you could just happen across Frank Lloyd Wright's space-age rotunda, your eyes would pop out of their sockets, but it's the planet's best-known modern building, so you are prepared. Don't forget the museum inside.

Museum of architecture This is the great Frank Lloyd Wright's only New York building, his 'Pantheon', as he called it. It was commissioned by Solomon R Guggenheim at the urging of his longtime friend and taste tutor, Baroness Hilla Rebay von Ehrenwiesen, though the incredibly wealthy metal-mining magnate died ten years before it was completed in 1959. The giant white nautilus is certainly arresting, but it's the interior that unleashes the most superlatives. Take the lift up to the top level, and slowly snake your way down the museum's spiral ramp to see why. This means that you can study the exhibits, look over the parapet to the lobby below, and finish up where you began without ever losing your way.

Museum of art There are something like 6,000 pieces in the Guggenheim Foundation's possession. Solomon R and his wife Irene Rothschild abandoned the Old Masters they sought at first, when Hilla Rebay introduced them to Kandinsky, Mondrian and Moholy-Nagy, Léger, Chagall and Gleizes, and they got hooked on the moderns. See also the early Picassos in the small rotunda and the 1992 tower extension, and, if you like the Impressionists and Post-Impressionists, look for the Thannhauser Collection, donated to the museum by art dealer Joseph K Thannhauser and always on display – unlike the Guggenheim holdings, which are rotated. The museum also stages special exhibitions, often focusing on the work of an individual artist.

HIGHLIGHTS

- The building
- *L'Hermitage à Pontoise,* Pissaro
- *Paris Through the Window,* Chagall
- *Woman Ironing,* Picasso
- *Nude,* Modigliani
- Kandinskys
- Klees
- Légers
- The shop

INFORMATION

- ✚ G2
- ✉ 1071 Fifth Avenue (88th Street)
- ☎ 212/423 3500
- 🕐 Fri–Wed 10–8. Closed 25 Dec, 1 Jan
- 🍴 Café
- Ⓜ 4, 5, 6 86th Street
- 🚌 M1, M2, M3, M4
- ♿ Good
- 💲 Inexpensive
- ↔ Central Park (➤ 40), Whitney Museum of American Art (➤ 42), Metropolitan Museum of Art (➤ 44)
- ❓ Lecture programme

23

COOPER-HEWITT DESIGN MUSEUM

HIGHLIGHTS

- Panelling in the hall
- Solarium
- Garden
- Architectural drawings
- Summer concerts
- Textiles
- Exhibitions

INFORMATION

- G2
- 2 E91st Street
- 212/860 6868
- Tue 10–9; Wed–Sat 10–5; Sun noon–5. Closed holidays
- None
- 4, 5, 6 86th Street
- M1, M2, M3, M4
- Good
- Inexpensive
- Central Park (➤ 40), Guggenheim (➤ 45)
- Tours available

The charming Cooper-Hewitt Design Museum collections are housed in an elegant, wood-panelled mansion. When snow falls in the holiday season, there's nowhere better to indulge in mawkishly nostalgic reveries.

Carnegie-Hewitt The mansion belonged to industrialist Andrew Carnegie, who, in 1903, had asked architects Babb, Cook & Willard for 'the most modest, plainest, and most roomy house in New York City'. This he did not receive (aside from the roominess), since this little château was built with modern conveniences galore – air conditioning and lifts – and a big gated garden to keep out the squatter neighbours. The entire neighbourhood came to be known as Carnegie Hill, thanks to his early patronage. Andrew's wife, Louise, lived here till her death in 1946, then, some 20 years later, the Carnegie Corporation donated it to the Smithsonian Institution to house the Hewitt sisters' collections. Still following? The three sisters, Amy, Eleanor and Sarah, had become infatuated with London's museums in 1897, and this set them off on their lifelong collecting spree.

And Cooper The girls' grandpa was Peter Cooper, founder of the Cooper Union college of art and architecture, and he offered the collection a home there, where it stayed until 1967. The contemporary Cooper-Hewitt is a vibrant institution where all kinds of event are happening. In addition to the collections, some of which are on display (though it's hard to predict which), there are various reference resources, including the country's biggest architectural drawings collection, a textile library with a 3,000-year span, auction catalogues, wallpapers, jewellery, earthenware – you name it.

Top: the former residence of the industrialist Andrew Carnegie and home to the Cooper-Hewitt Museum

YANKEE STADIUM

Final out, bottom of the ninth and, whether the home team has won or lost, Sinatra's 'New York, New York' wafts over the blue seats. Baseball embodies the American spirit: this stadium is New York.

What baseball means New Yorkers are sports mad, even though a team nowadays is almost more a brand name than a group of athletes. Professional baseball today is a big-bucks business, which reached its apogee of heartlessness with the players' strike of 1994. To Yankee fans – already licking wounds inflicted by unpopular team owner, George Steinbrenner – this signaled the end of baseball, and thus of America. Their 1996 and 1998 World Series victories, however, made the world turn again.

The house that Ruth built If you want to see what makes the New Yorker tick (unless his or her heart belongs to the 1962 upstart National League NY Mets), go to see a Yankees home game. The Yankees dominated the early eras of baseball. In 1920 Babe Ruth joined the team and quickly became a hero of such mythic stature that his popularity built them a stadium in 1923 (renovated in the mid-1970s).

Where have you gone, Joe Di Maggio? The Babe's No. 3 is only one of the 'retired' numbers that honor great players who bore them and that will never be re-allocated. Lou Gehrig was No. 4; No. 5 was Joe Di Maggio (he who married Marilyn Monroe and pulled off a 56-game hitting streak); No. 7 was Mickey Mantle, and No. 8 was Yogi Berra. These four played between 1946 and 1960, when the team won eight World Series titles – they are why Yankee fans 'bleed pinstripes'.

HIGHLIGHTS

- The 1998 team
- Bleachers (cheap seats)
- Seventh Inning Stretch
- Eddie Layton, organist
- 'Giveaway Days'

INFORMATION

- ✚ Off map
- ✉ E161st Street, Bronx
- ☎ 718/293 4300.
  Ticketmaster 212/307 1212
- 🕐 Season runs Apr–Oct. Check schedule for home games
- 🍴 Concession stands
- Ⓜ 4, D, C (weekdays) 161st Street
- 🚌 BX6, BX13, BX55
- ♿ Good
- 💲 Expensive

47

25

THE CLOISTERS

- Unicorn Tapestries
- Fuentidueña Chapel
- Cuxa Cloister
- Saint Guilhem Cloister
- Annunciation Altarpiece
- Boppard stained glass
- Rosary bead carved with the Passion
- Bonnefont Cloister herb garden
- Ramparts – views to Hudson

INFORMATION

- Off map at F1
- Fort Tryon Park, North Manhattan
- 718/923 3700
- Nov–Feb: Tue–Sun 9:30–4:45. Mar–Oct: Tue–Sun 9:30–5:15. Closed holidays
- A 190th Street
- M4
- Good
- Inexpensive
- Tours Tue–Fri 3; Sun noon. Joint same-day admission with the Met. Concert programme of live and recorded medieval music

A 12th-century Spanish apse attached to a Romanesque cloister and a Gothic chapel – what's all this doing in the Bronx? This is the Met's medieval branch: the incongruity is hallucinogenic, and amazing enough in itself, but the sights are just heavenly.

Medieval world The building in Fort Tryon Park – a site in the far north of Manhattan Island that was donated by Rockefeller Jr. – is not medieval, you'll be astonished to learn, but there are plenty of parts of buildings inside it that are. The 12th-century pink stone Cuxa Cloister was liberated from the French Pyrenees, and the 3,000 lime-stone blocks of the Fuentidueña Chapel apse were rescued from the ruins of the church of Saint-Martín in Spain. The Cloisters are not some Disney-esque simulacrum of medieval Europe, however. Being able to gaze at the ribbed vaulting of the late-Romanesque Pontaut Chapter House, or strolling past the early-Flemish Annunciation Altarpiece of Robert Campin to the familiar 15th-century Unicorn Tapestries, are treats that have not been possible in Europe since the Age of Chivalry exhibition at London's Royal Academy gathered together high points of medieval art some years ago.

Through the ages The collections are arranged chronologically, so that one can trace not only the metamorphosis of architectural styles, but also of the medieval mind – by turns awestruck, playful, bawdy and terrified. The bulk of the art and architecture was amassed by sculptor George Gray Bernard early this century. Much was rescued from ruin: the effigy of the Crusader, Jean d'Alluye, for instance, was doing duty as a bridge, while the priceless Unicorn Tapestries were once draped over fruit trees as frost blankets.

NEW YORK's
best

BUILDINGS

Reach for the sky

The tallest building in the world is the Sears Roebuck Tower in Chicago, but in their day the following New York structures were the highest: Park Row Building (1899–1908, 386 feet), Chrysler Building (1929–30, 1,048 feet), Empire State Building (1930–72, 1,250 feet), World Trade Center Towers (1972–79, 1,350 feet). Contrary to popular myth, the Flatiron was never the tallest.

The Lower Manhattan skyline, dominated by the twin towers of the World Trade Center

CATHEDRAL OF ST JOHN THE DIVINE
Started in 1892 and not finished yet, this would be the world's biggest.
✚ Off map at G1 ✉ Amsterdam Avenue (W112th Street) ☎ 212/316 7540 ⏰ Mon–Sat 7–5; Sun 7AM–8PM 🚇 1, 9 110th Street

CITICORP CENTER
The 45-degree lightbox is one of the skyline's greatest hits at night. The four-legged base shelters St Peter's Church and the great atrium.
✚ F6 ✉ 153 E53rd Street 🚇 6 51st Street

THE DAKOTA
First of the great Upper West Side luxury apartment houses, designed by Henry Hardenberg, but famous as John Lennon's murder site.
✚ E3 ✉ 1 W72nd Street (Central Park West) 🚇 B, C 72nd Street

FLATIRON BUILDING
1902 skyscraper named after its amazing shape: an isosceles triangle with a sharp angle pointing uptown.
🔼 D8 ✉ 175 Fifth Avenue (E22nd/23rd Streets) 🚇 N, R 23rd Street

LEVER HOUSE
The Seagram and this 1952 Skidmore, Owings & Merrill building were precursors of all glass blocks.
🔼 E5 ✉ 390 Park Avenue (53rd/54th Streets) ☎ 212/960 4685 🕐 Lobby Mon–Fri 10–5; Sun 1–5 🚇 E, F Fifth Avenue

'LIPSTICK BUILDING'
This likeable 1986 show-off is by John Burgee with Philip Johnson.
🔼 F5 ✉ 885 Third Avenue (55th/56th Streets) 🚇 6 51st Street

METLIFE BUILDING
Known to New Yorkers as the Pan Am Building – which it was until 1981 – it's by Bauhaus priest Walter Gropius, plus Emery Roth & Sons and Pietro Belluschi.
🔼 E6 ✉ 200 Park Avenue (44th–45th Streets) 🚇 4, 5, 6, 7 42nd Street

NY STOCK EXCHANGE
Neoclassical façade dates only from 1903. See trading from the gallery and recall the Crash of 1929.
🔼 A13 ✉ 20 Broad Street ☎ 212/656 5167 🕐 Mon–Fri 9:15–4 🚇 2, 3, 4, 5 Wall Street; 1, 9 Rector Street; J, M, Z Broad Street ✋ Free

The Flatiron Building was one of the first structures to be erected around a steel frame – the basic support of every subsequent skyscraper

SEAGRAM BUILDING
Mies van der Rohe's 1958 bronze glazed tower is *the* Modernist landmark. Philip Johnson interiors.
🔼 E5–E6 ✉ 375 Park Avenue (52nd/53rd Streets) ☎ 212/572 7000 🕐 Tour Tue 3PM 🍴 Two 🚇 E, F Fifth Avenue ✋ Free

TRUMP TOWER
'Glitzy' captured in pink marble and glass.
🔼 E5 ✉ 725 Fifth Avenue (56th Street) ☎ 212/832 2000 🕐 8AM–10PM 🍴 Several 🚇 E, F Fifth Avenue

UNITED NATIONS HEADQUARTERS
Officially outside the USA, this vast 1947–63 complex included Le Corbusier among its architects. 🔼 F6–F7 ✉ First Avenue (45th Street) ☎ 212/963 7713 🕐 Fri–Wed 9:15–4:45. Closed weekends Jan–Feb, 1 Jan, 25 Dec 🍴 Café and restaurant 🚇 4, 5, 6, 7 42nd Street, Grand Central ✋ Free

WORLD FINANCIAL CENTER
Cesar Pelli's waterfront World Trade Center neighbour includes the fab Winter Garden atrium.
🔼 A12 ✉ 200 Liberty Street ☎ 212/945 0505 🍴 Several 🚇 1, 9, N, R Cortlandt Street; A, C, E Chambers Street; 4, 5 Fulton Street ✋ Free

OF THE OLD

> **See Top 25 Sights for**
> **FRICK MANSION (► 41)**
> **SCHERMERHORN ROW,**
> **SOUTH STREET SEAPORT (► 27)**

St Patrick's Cathedral

BLOCK BEAUTIFUL
This picturesque, tree-lined 1920s row really is called this. Also see the pretty square nearby, centred on private Gramercy Park (► 54).
🚇 D8 ✉ E19th Street (Irving Place/Third Avenue) 🚊 N, R 14th Street Union Square; 6 23rd Street

CITY HALL
French Renaissance-style façade and elegant Georgian interior – see it by visiting the Governor's Room, with a small furniture museum.
🚇 B12 ✉ Broadway (Murray Street) ☎ 212/788 3000 🕐 Mon–Fri 10–3:30 🚊 2, 3 Park Place; 4, 5, 6 Brooklyn Bridge/City Hall; N, R City Hall 🆓 Free

ST PATRICK'S CATHEDRAL
James Renwick's Gothic Revival cathedral is the US's biggest for Catholics.
🚇 E5–E6 ✉ Fifth Avenue (50th Street) ☎ 212/753 2261 🕐 6AM–9PM 🚊 6 51st Street; E, F Fifth Avenue

SINGER BUILDING & HAUGHWOUT STORE
Two of the best ambassadors for the SoHo Cast Iron Historic District (► 54) – the 26 blocks of skyscraper forerunners, now galleries and posh boutiques. The Haughwout had the first Otis steam lift.
🚇 C10 ✉ Singer: 561 Broadway. Haughwout: 488 Broadway 🚊 N, R Prince Street; B, D, F, Q Broadway/Lafayette

WASHINGTON SQUARE: 'THE ROW' AND ARCH
'The Row' (1–13 North side) housed movers and shakers of early 19th-century New York City – read Henry James's *Washington Square* for details.
🚇 C9 ✉ South end of Fifth Avenue 🚊 N, R 8th Street; A, C, E, B, D, F, Q W4th Street

WOOLWORTH BUILDING
The world's tallest until the Chrysler, Cass Gilbert's Gothic beauty has NYC's richest lobby – see witty bas reliefs of architect and tycoon.
🚇 B12 ✉ 233 Broadway 🕐 Lobby Mon–Fri 7–6. Closed holidays 🚊 2, 3 Park Place; N, R City Hall

Literary New York
Old New York is the title of a collection of Edith Wharton novellas that brings to life the *Age of Innocence* (the Wharton novel filmed by Scorsese). The other chronicler of 19th-century New York manners was, of course, Henry James, especially in *Washington Square* (filmed as *The Heiress*). For the jazz age of the 1920s, read F Scott Fitzgerald's short stories.

VIEWS

BROOKLYN HEIGHTS ESPLANADE

As traffic clogs the Brooklyn–Queens Expressway beneath your feet, all is serene on this elegantissimo promenade, with some of New York's most covetable houses and rare gardens at your back, and Manhattan's financial centre spread out before you.

✚ Off map at C14   ✉ West end of Clark Street   🚇 2, 3 Clark Street

PARK AVENUE FROM CARNEGIE HILL

The view from here to the MetLife building is best experienced during the Christmas holiday season when pine trees bedecked with sparkling white lights bisect the route.

✚ G2   🚇 6 86th Street, 96th Street

ROOSEVELT ISLAND TRAMWAY

One of New York City's oddities is this Swiss-made cable car that has been flying passengers to the site of the NYC Lunatic Asylum (undergoing restoration) and on into Queens since 1976.

✚ F5   ✉ Second Avenue (60th Street)   ☎ 212/832 4543
🕐 Mon–Fri 6AM–2AM; weekends 6AM–3AM   🚇 B, Q Lexington Avenue
💲 Inexpensive

STATEN ISLAND FERRY

Those three words 'Staten Island Ferry' are nearly always followed by these three: 'city's best bargain'. The voyage is like a tiny holiday.

✚ A14   ✉ Whitehall Terminal
☎ 212/806 6901 or 718/390 5253   🕐 24-hour service
🚇 N, R Whitehall Street South Ferry   💲 Free

WORLD FINANCIAL CENTER (➤ 51)

Join the Wall Street hordes in the piazza for sunset over the Hudson.

A table with a view

This is a sought-after commodity. Eat well (and pay handsome sums) at Brooklyn's River Café (✉ 1 Water Street ☎ 718/522 2000) or the Water's Edge in Queens (✉ 44th Drive, East River, Long Island City ☎ 718/482 0033), with its free boat taxi and floor-to-ceiling windows. The Water Club (✉ 500 E30th Street ☎ 212/683 3333) has the view in the other direction, and new American food. Or dine waterside at the Boathouse Café (☎ 212/517 2233) on Central Park's lake.

Lower Manhattan and the East River viewed from Brooklyn Heights

NEIGHBOURHOODS

TriBeCa

**See Top 25 Sights for
CHINATOWN (► 30)
GREENWICH VILLAGE (► 31)**

EAST VILLAGE

Somewhat tamer than it used to be but if you're over 30 and not in black, you'll still feel odd.

D10–E10 🚇 F Second Avenue; 6 Astor Place

GRAMERCY PARK AND FLATIRON

The former – peaceful and pleasant to stroll – is centred on the eponymous park; the latter on the eponymous building (► 51). It's grown out of the photography district, and now contains 'Silicon Alley' plus the Restaurant Row on Park Avenue South.

🚇 D8 🚇 N, R, 6 23rd Street

LITTLE ITALY

Reduced to Mulberry Street, this is a nice place to stroll and café hop. Skip the touristy red-sauce spaghetterias, and see Scorsese's *Mean Streets* for the real thing. Adjacent streets have become the latest trendy area and have been dubbed 'Nolita' – North of Little Italy.

🚇 C10–C11 🚇 6 Spring Street

LOWER EAST SIDE

Where the melting pot landed; birth of Jewish New York: Orchard Street.

🚇 D/E11–D/E12 🚇 F Delancey Street

SOHO

South of Houston (say '*How*-stun') saw 1980s art mania, when its gorgeous cast-iron framed buildings were 'loft-ised' on the cheap. Now it's for chain-store shopping, gallery-hopping and crowd-fighting.

🚇 B10–C10 🚇 N, R Prince Street; C, E Spring Street

THEATRE/GARMENT DISTRICT

As it sounds. It is delineated more or less by Sixth and Ninth Avenues and 34th to 59th Streets, with theatres clustering on Broadway, and the 'garmentos' – those who work in the fashion trade – along Seventh Avenue.

🚇 D5–D6; C6–D6 🚇 N, R, 1, 2, 3 Times Square

TRIBECA

Like SoHo, the Flatiron and the East Village, the 'Triangle Below Canal' was designated a neighbourhood by real estate agents, but the sobriquet stuck. Once a windy wasteland of warehouses, now it has many top tables (Montrachet, Nobu, Chanterelle), plus rich architects, artists and filmmakers in lofts.

🚇 A10–B10 🚇 A, 1, 2, 3 Chambers Street

The East Village

Not so much a neighbourhood as a state of mind – the one that parents hope is just a phase and which requires pierced lips, nipples and navels and tons of tattoos. The streets themselves are bursting with cheap and good restaurants, divey bars, coffee lounges, vintage clothing stores and wholefood emporia. Pretty Tompkins Square Park has great concerts in summer.

MUSEUMS

Musical soirées

At major museums this is an innovation catching on quickly. The Metropolitan Museum of Art started the whole thing, and among those to have jumped on the bandwagon are the Guggenheim, with jazz in Frank Lloyd Wright's rotunda; the Metropolitan's Cloisters outpost; and the Frick, with chamber music in its beautiful courtyard.

FORBES MAGAZINE GALLERIES
Toy soldiers, Fabergé eggs, plus art.
✚ C9 ✉ 63 Fifth Avenue (12th Street) ☎ 212/206–5548
🕐 Tue, Wed, Fri, Sat 10–4 🚇 4, 5, 6 14th Street 💵 Free

JEWISH MUSEUM
Chronicling Jewish experience worldwide, with artefacts from 4,000 years.
✚ G2 ✉ 1109 Fifth Avenue ☎ 212/423 3200
🕐 Sun–Thu 11–5:45; Tue 11–8 🍽 Café 🚇 4, 5, 6 86th Street
💵 Moderate

LOWER EAST SIDE TENEMENT MUSEUM
A reconstruction of life in this 1863 tenement block, plus talks and tours.
✚ D11 ✉ 97 Orchard Street ☎ 212/431 0233
🕐 Tue–Fri 11–4; Sun 10–5 🚇 F, J, M, Z Delancey Street; B, D, Q Grand Street 💵 Inexpensive

NEW MUSEUM OF CONTEMPORARY ART
What MoMA stops at, Whitney shows; where Whitney balks, this museum starts.
✚ C10 ✉ 583 Broadway (Houston/Prince Streets)
☎ 212/219 1222 🕐 Wed–Sun noon–6; Sat noon–8
🚇 N, R Prince Street 💵 Inexpensive

NEW YORK CITY FIRE MUSEUM
See the firefighting dog! Pretty *beaux-arts* station.
✚ B10 ✉ 278 Spring Street, SoHo ☎ 212/691 1303 🕐 Tue–Sat 10–4 🚇 C, E Spring Street 💵 Contribution

PIERPONT MORGAN LIBRARY
McKim, Mead & White's 1902 *palazzo* for Morgan's sublime manuscripts.
✚ D7–E7 ✉ 29 E36th Street ☎ 212/685 0008 🕐 Tue–Sat 10:30–5; Sun 1–5 🚇 6 33rd Street 💵 Moderate

MUSEUM OF JEWISH HERITAGE: A LIVING MEMORIAL TO THE HOLOCAUST
Changing exhibits of memorabilia and history.
✚ A14 ✉ 18 First Place, Battery Park City ☎ 212/962 1800
🕐 Sun–Wed 9–5; Thu 9–8; Fri 9–2 🚇 1,9 Rector Street 💵 Inexpensive

New York City Fire Museum

GALLERIES & OUTDOOR ART

Red Cube, by Isamu
Noguchi, Church Street

Outside art

Save time and combine art with
sightseeing.

Stabile (1971), Alexander Calder
✚ A12 ✉ 6 World Trade
Center

Group of Four Trees (1972),
Jean Dubuffet
✚ B12 ✉ Chase Manhattan
Bank, Pine/Nassau/Liberty
Streets

Gay Liberation (1980), George
Segal
✚ B9 ✉ Christopher Park,
Sheridan Square

Prometheus (1934), Paul
Manship
✚ E5 ✉ Rockefeller Center

Single Form (1964), Barbara
Hepworth
✚ F7 ✉ Pool of Secretariat
Building, UN, First Avenue (46th
Street)

Reclining Figure (1965), Henry
Moore
✚ D4 ✉ Reflecting Pool,
Lincoln Center

Night Presence IV (1972),
Louise Nevelson
✚ G2 ✉ Park Avenue (92nd
Street)

SOHO GALLERIES
Doing the SoHo galleries, brunch and shopping (in a
different order of importance) is one version of the
quintessential New York Saturday. The following
galleries are worth a look. Call for the current
showing times. ⊕ Generally Tue–Sat 11–6 Ⓜ N, R Prince
Street; C, E Spring Street

The Drawing Center	✉ 35 Wooster Street	☎ 212/219 2166
Gagosian	✉ 136 Wooster Street	☎ 212/228 2878
Lehmann Maupin	✉ 39 Greene Street	☎ 212/965 0753
Leo Castelli	✉ 420 W Broadway	☎ 212/431 5160
Meisel	✉ 141 Prince Street	☎ 212/677 1340
Sonnabend	✉ 420 W Broadway	☎ 212/966 6160
Vorpal	✉ 459 W Broadway	☎ 212/777 3939
Thread Waxing Space	✉ 476 Broadway	☎ 212/966 9520

CHELSEA GALLERIES
The new art district is way west.

Dia Center for the Arts	✉ 548 W22nd Street	☎ 212/989 5566
Greene Nafrali	✉ 526 W26th Street	☎ 212/463 7770
Marks	✉ 522 W22nd Street	☎ 212/243 1650
Paula Cooper	✉ 534 W21st Street	☎ 212/255 1105
Rupert Goldsworthy	✉ 453 W17th Street	☎ 212/414 4560
White Columns	✉ 320 W13th Street	☎ 212/924 4212

UPTOWN GALLERIES
Dressier than Chelsea or SoHo viewing.

Gagosian	✉ 980 Madison Avenue	☎ 212/744 2313
Marlborough	✉ 40 W57th Street	☎ 212/541 4900
Mary Boone	✉ 745 Fifth Avenue	☎ 212/752 2929
Pace	✉ 32 E57th Street	☎ 212/421 3292

FOR KIDS

See Top 25 Sights for

BRONX ZOO

The biggest city zoo in the US, 100 years old in 1999, has 4,000 animals, a children's zoo, and monorail. Don't miss the newest attraction, the $43 million Congo Gorilla Forest.
➕ Off map at H1 ✉ Fordham Road (Bronx River Parkway Northeast) ☎ 718/367 1010 ⏰ Apr–Oct: 10–5. Nov–Mar: 10–4:30 🍴 Restaurant 🚇 2, 5 Pelham Parkway 🎟 Moderate

CHILDREN'S MUSEUM OF THE ARTS

Highlights: the Monet Ballpond, Architects Alley and the Wonder Theater.
➕ C11 ✉ 182 Lafayette Street ☎ 212/274 0986 ⏰ Thu–Sun 12–5; Wed 12–7 🚇 6 Spring Street 🎟 Moderate

CHILDREN'S MUSEUM OF MANHATTAN

Ignore the word 'museum' – here they can make their own TV show.
➕ D5 ✉ 212 W83rd Street ☎ 212/721 1234 ⏰ Sep–May: Wed, Thu 1:30–5:30; Fri–Sun 10–5. Jun–Aug: Wed–Sun 10–5 🚇 1, 9, B, C 86th Street 🎟 Moderate

FAO SCHWARZ

The world's most famous toyshop—see the movie *Big*; set advance spending and time limits. The giant singing clock at the entrance is scary.
➕ E5 ✉ 767 Fifth Avenue ☎ 212/644 9400 ⏰ Mon–Sat 9–9; Sun 10–8 🚇 E, F Fifth Avenue; 4, 6 59th Street 🎟 Free

HARLEY DAVIDSON CAFÉ AND PLANET HOLLYWOOD

Two shameless pack-em-in theme restaurants that ten-year-olds adore.
➕ E5 ✉ 1370 Sixth Avenue (W 56th Street); 140 W 57th Street ☎ 212/245 6000; 212/333 7827 ⏰ Daily till late 🚇 N, R, B, Q 57th Street 🎟 Moderate

STATEN ISLAND CHILDREN'S MUSEUM

It is a bit of a trek, but there is always something going on here.
➕ Off map ✉ Snug Harbor, 1000 Richmond Terrace, Staten Island ☎ 718/273 2060 ⏰ Tue–Sun 12–5 🚇 Ferry to Staten Island, then S40 bus 🎟 Moderate

Kids' Broadway

All over town are theatrical troupes dedicated to the entertainment of youth.

The Paper Bag Players
Perform at Sylvia and Danny Kaye Playhouse
✉ 68th Street (Park/Lexington Avenues) ☎ 212/772 4448

New York Youth Theater
✉ 593 Park Avenue (64th Street) ☎ 212/242 2822

Theaterworks/USA
✉ Broadway (76th Street) ☎ 212/647 7373

Free Things

On parade

New York loves a parade, and nobody does it more often than New Yorkers.

St Patrick's Day Parade
✉ Fifth Avenue (44th–86th Streets) 🕐 17 Mar

Easter Parade ✉ Fifth Avenue (44th–59th Streets) 🕐 Easter Sun

Lesbian and Gay Pride Day Parade ✉ Fifth Avenue

Street entertainment: a sound return for a small investment

(Columbus Circle–Washington Square) 🕐 Late June

Columbus Day Parade
✉ Fifth Avenue (44th–86th Streets) 🕐 12 Oct

Halloween Parade
✉ Greenwich Village
🕐 31 Oct

Macy's Thanksgiving Day Parade ✉ Central Park West (79th Street)–Broadway (34th Street) 🕐 Fourth Thu in Nov

See Top 25 Sights for
CENTRAL PARK (► 40)
COOPER-HEWITT (TUE EVENING FREE, ► 46)
FULTON FISH MARKET, SOUTH STREET SEAPORT (► 27)
GUGGENHEIM (THU 6–8PM PAY-WHAT-YOU-WISH, ► 45)
MUSEUM OF MODERN ART (THU 5–9PM PAY-WHAT-YOU-WISH, ► 38)
NEW YORK PUBLIC LIBRARY (► 34)

BEING ON TV
Write in advance for free tickets to talk shows.
✉ NBC, 30 Rockefeller Plaza ☎ 212/664 3056 🚇 B, D, F 47th–50th Streets

BIG APPLE GREETERS
Volunteers who like showing off their city will take you places in NYC (free; 48 hours' notice required).
☎ 212/669 3602/8273

BROOKLYN BOTANIC GARDEN
A 52-acre expanse with herbs, roses, fragrant flora especially for the blind, and Shakespeare, kids' and Japanese gardens.
➕ Off map at F14 ✉ 1000 Washington Avenue ☎ 718/622 4433 🕐 Apr–Sep: Tue–Fri 8–6; weekends 10–6. Oct–Mar: Tue–Fri 8–4:30; weekends 10–4:30 🍴 Café 🚇 2, 3 Eastern Parkway

BRYANT PARK
The summer evening 'walk in' movies are a new tradition; also concerts.
➕ D6 🚇 B, D, F, 42nd Street

FORBES MAGAZINE GALLERIES (► 55)

NY STOCK EXCHANGE GALLERY (► 51)

SOHO AND CHELSEA GALLERY-HOPPING (► 56)

STATEN ISLAND FERRY (► 53)
(50-cent round-trip counts as free.)

WALKING
The world's best walking city. You'll need around two minutes per block, comfortable shoes and sunglasses.

WASHINGTON SQUARE (► 52)
In summer it's live theatre – literally. Genuinely funny stand-ups perform.

WORLD FINANCIAL CENTER (► 51)
The Winter Garden Atrium has events year round.

GYMS

CHELSEA PIERS SPORTS CENTER
Egalitarian, vast, packed with a four-tier golf range, two ice-skating rinks, marina, climbing wall, track and field arena and big swimming pool.
B7 ✉ Piers 59–62 West Side Highway ☎ 212/336 6666 🚇 C, E, 23rd Street

CRUNCH
Cyberpunk styling, gimmicks (live DJs, haircutting, heart-rate monitors).
D9 ✉ 54 E13th Street (and other branches) ☎ 212/475 2018 🚇 N, R, 4, 6 Union Square

EQUINOX
Everyone's good looking, and a fair bit of eyeing goes on – but what the heck, those bodies took a lot of hard work.
D3 ✉ 897 Broadway (and other branches) ☎ 212/780 9300 🚇 N, R 23rd Street

JIVAMUKTI YOGA CENTER
Without a doubt, the trendiest ashram in town.
C9 ✉ 6 Astor Place, 404 Lafayette Street ☎ 212/353 0214 🚇 B, D, F, Q Broadway/Lafayette

PRINTING HOUSE
A friendly sort of place with classes, a rooftop pool, squash courts and a sundeck.
B9 ✉ 421 Hudson Street ☎ 212/243 7600 🚇 1, 2, 3, 9 Houston Street

REEBOK SPORTS CLUB NY
Everything from ski and windsurfing simulators to fancy bistro and huge prices.
D4 ✉ 160 Columbus Avenue ☎ 212/362 6800 🚇 1, 2, 3, 9 66th Street

VANDERBILT YMCA
Classes, two good pools and no snooty attitude.
F6 ✉ 224 E47th Street ☎ 212/756 9600 🚇 6 51st Street

WORLD
Half spiritual haven, half professional iron-pumper's heaven – it's light and spacious, and it's open 24 hours.
D3 ✉ 1926 Broadway ☎ 212/874 0942 🚇 1, 2, 3, 9 66th Street

Where do you work out?

Many of the things people used to do at frenetic all-night dance clubs – meet, sweat, schmooze, pose – are now accomplished at the gym. All New Yorkers have gym membership. Most use it. 'Where do you work out?' is a perfectly reasonable question, as unsurprising as the sight of people bouncing rhythmically in upstairs windows. Or, more likely, doing their sun salutations, since yoga is the favourite obsession.

The New York gym provides more than just exercise, it's a way of life

'ONLY IN NEW YORK'

BARNEY'S WAREHOUSE SALE

Warehouse sales are known elsewhere, but you must understand, Barney's is *the* store where every single New Yorker bar none aspires to shop for clothes. Consequently, *everyone* goes to this event. It is a zoo.

⊞ C8 ⊠ 255 W17th Street ◷ Feb, Sep 🚇 1 18th Street

BASKETBALL STARS ON THE STREET

At 'The Cage', you can see basketball played by *future* stars, as good as the pros (and it's free).

⊞ B10 ⊠ Sixth Avenue (W3rd Street) 🚇 A, B, C, D, E, F W 4th Street

GRAND MARCH OF THE DACHSHUNDS

This is the climax of the two-hour Dachshund Octoberfest (usually the third Saturday at noon). The short-legged dogs parade around the fountain.

⊞ C9 ⊠ Washington Square Park 🚇 N, R, 8th Street

HOWARD STERN

If he didn't invent the genre of 'shock jock', this irritating, self-consciously controversial individual certainly popularised it. To hear him, tune in to FM 92.3 WXRK, Monday to Friday mornings.

Macy's Thanksgiving Day Parade

MACY'S THANKSGIVING DAY PARADE BALLOON INFLATION

Macy's Thanksgiving Day Parade is a real treat, but better are the impromptu street parties that convene the night before, as the balloons go up.

⊞ E2 ⊠ Central Park West around 81st Street 🚇 C 81st Street

POETRY SLAMS

These are competitive poetry readings. One night a week (Friday is normal at this place), writers declaim, chant, even sing their work to raucous crowds.

⊞ D10 ⊠ Nuyorican Poets Café, 236 E3rd Street (Avenues B/C) ☎ 212/505 8183 🚇 F Second Avenue

RUSSIAN BATHS

This has been here forever and looks that way in the Stone Room, hot as hell, where you get your schwitze – a beating with soapy oak leaves.

⊞ D10 ⊠ 268 E10th Street ☎ 212/473 8806 🚇 6 Astor Place

Wigstock

This fab Labor Day fest is as it sounds – an excuse to wear wild wigs, wild drag and dish. RuPaul started here. Started in 1984, it has now outgrown its venue.

NEW YORK
where to...

HAUTE CUISINE

Prices

Expect to pay per person for a meal, excluding drink

£££	over $50
££	$30–50
£	up to $30

Brunch

It's hard to imagine what New Yorkers did before the invention of brunch. These days the weekend noontime meal can be everything from the basic omelette to a multi-course culinary adventure. The following are some perennial favourites. Go early or late to avoid the crowds

Sarabeth's

✉ Hotel Wales, 1295 Madison Avenue ☎ 212/410 7335

Bubby's

✉ 120 Hudson Street
☎ 212/219 0666

Petite Abeille

✉ 466 Hudson Street
☎ 212/741 6479

Time Cafe

✉ 2330 Broadway
☎ 212/579 5100

Tea & Sympathy

✉ 108 Greenwich Avenue
☎ 212/807 8329

CAFÉ BOULUD £££

No jacket is required at this 'casual' restaurant but the experience is no less exquisite. The inspired cooking provides four distinct menus – traditional French, seasonal, vegetarian and foods of the world.

✚ F4 ✉ Surrey Hotel, 20 E 76th Street (Fifth/Madison Avenues) ☎ 212/772 2600 ◷ Closed Sun, Mon lunch ◉ 6 77th Street

CHANTERELLE £££

Serene restaurant on a quiet TriBeCa corner. Billowy curtains, lovely flower arrangements and elegant tables provide the perfect backdrop for a romantic evening. Seafood sausage is a dish to dream on and the simple desserts can linger on the palate for hours.

✚ B11 ✉ 2 Harrison Street (Hudson Street) ☎ 212/966 6960 ◷ Closed Sun, Mon lunch ◉ 1, 9 Franklin Street

DANIEL £££

Perhaps the most formal restaurant in the city, from the gold leaf inscription over the carved doors to the columned arches. Exquisitely restrained, modern French dishes – opt for the *degustation* menu to fully appreciate the chef's brilliance.

✚ F3 ✉ E76th Street (Fifth/Madison Avenues) ☎ 212/288 0033 ◷ Closed Sun ◉ 6 77th Street

JEAN-GEORGES £££

Everything about this restaurant radiates an indulgent urban elegance in a sleek, formal dining room known for creative food and impeccable service. Don't miss the caramelized cauliflower with raisin and caper sauce.

✚ D4 ✉ Trump International Hotel, 1 Central Park West (60th/61st Streets) ☎ 212/299 3900 ◷ Closed Sat, Sun lunch ◉ A, C, 1, 9, B, D Columbus Circle

LE CIRQUE 2000 £££

A veritable circus of the stars; Le Cirque 2000 is the city's pre-eminent spot to see and be seen. The decor defies description – think Versailles meets Disney – and the food strives for greatness.

✚ E6 ✉ New York Palace Hotel, 455 Madison Avenue (51st Street) ☎ 212/794 9292 ◷ Closed Sun ◉ 6 51st Street

LUTÈCE £££

This venerable restaurant defined fine French cuisine when it opened over 35 years ago. The new regime has made changes – lightening and contemporising the food and the decor– but classics like the terrine of foie gras are as luscious as the more modern cuisine.

✚ F6 ✉ 249 E50th Street (Second/Third Avenues) ☎ 212/752 2225 ◷ Closed Mon, Sat lunch, Sun ◉ 6 51st Street

MARCH £££

Be seduced by this romantic restaurant that coddles each diner with attentive service. The menu maintains a delicate balance between restrained cooking and wild culinary innovation. Meals are all prix fixe.

✚ G5 ✉ 405 E58th Street (First Avenue/Sutton Place) ☎ 212/754 6272 ◷ Closed lunch ◉ 4, 5, 6 59th Street

AMERICAN NOUVEAU

AUREOLE £££

Stunning and inventive American cuisine followed by artistically sculptural desserts that end every meal with a bang. Conservatively fashionable dining room bedecked with magnificent flower arrangements. Eating in the tiny outdoor garden is a treat.

🚇 F5 ✉ 34 E61st Street (Madison/Park Avenues) ☎ 212/319 1660 🕐 Closed Sat, Sun lunch 🚇 4 ,5 ,6 59th Street

CLEMENTINE ££

Feel the chic atmosphere as you pass through the beautiful bar crowd, slip into a leather booth and order one of the excellent cocktails. The front room sizzles with the unique buzz of New York, while the back room is quieter and more refined. Either way you will enjoy the inventive American fare.

🚇 C9 ✉ 1 Fifth Avenue (8th Street) ☎ 212/253 0003 🕐 Closed lunch 🚇 A, C, E, B, D, F W4th Street

GOTHAM BAR AND GRILL £££

This restaurant lives up to its name – befitting an urban megalopolis – and it epitomizes New York grandeur. World-class dishes like the rack of lamb with swiss chard and roasted shallots have delighted New Yorkers since 1984. The soaring space is light and airy with huge, modern chandeliers and classical accents.

🚇 C9 ✉ 12 E12th Street (Fifth Avenue) ☎ 212/620 4020 🕐 Closed Sat, Sun lunch 🚇 N, R, 4, 6 Union Square

MERCER KITCHEN ££-£££

An underground oasis of exposed brick, sleek lines, dim lighting and elegant accents – such as the orchid on each table. The scene is electric and the food lives up to the hype, with exquisitely casual offerings like wood grilled prawns with garlic confit terrine and pistou.

🚇 C10 ✉ Mercer Hotel, 99 Prince Street (Mercer Street) ☎ 212/966 5454 🕐 Daily 🚇 N, R Prince Street

PARK AVENUE CAFE £££

If you like to eat and laugh you will enjoy the whimsically delicious cooking of this thoroughly American bistro. Oysters served on a towering ice sculpture and a cage constructed of day-glo curry fries reflect the creativity of the kitchen.

🚇 F5 ✉ 100 E63rd Street (Lexington/Park Avenues) ☎ 212/644 1900 🕐 Daily 🚇 4, 5, 6 59th Street

VERITAS £££

Tiny restaurant distinguished by clean, natural lines, with one wall made of Italian tile, and another displaying pretty hand-blown vases. A world-class wine list – over 1,300 producers – is just one of the draws, and the contemporary menu runs from rich, soulful dishes like braised veal cheeks to Asian inspired salmon with greens and curry emulsion.

🚇 D8 ✉ 43 E20th Street (Broadway/Park Avenue South) ☎ 212/353 3700 🕐 Closed Sat, Sun lunch 🚇 6 23rd Street

Doing lunch

For Restaurant Week, each June, many of the better restaurants in the city offer a prix-fixe lunch in which the price corresponds to the year ($20.00 in the year 2000). Some of the restaurants continue the deal through Labor Day, and it is the best way to dine at serious restaurants for discount prices. Some of the annual favourites include: Felidia (➤ 67), Gotham Bar and Grill (➤ 63), Nobu (➤ 66), Le Cirque 2000 (➤ 62), Chanterelle (➤ 62), Aureole (➤ 63), Spartina (➤ 67), Café Boulud (➤ 62)

WORLD CUISINES

Bagel people

In many cities across the country you can find bagels in such bastardised flavours as blueberry, chocolate or apple crumb. Not so in any self-respecting bagel shop in New York. Bagels are a serious matter and they are debated fiercely – there are Ess-A people and there are H&H people. While these are the two reigning kings, there are a couple of others that are worth their salt, or poppy seeds, as the case may be.

H&H

✉ 2239 Broadway
☎ 212/595 8003

✉ 639 W46th Street
☎ 212/595 8000

Ess-A-Bagel

✉ 831 Third Avenue
☎ 212/980 1010

✉ 359 First Avenue
☎ 212/260 2252

Pick A Bagel

✉ 1101 Lexington Avenue
☎ 212/517 6500

✉ 200 W57th Street
☎ 212/957 5151

Columbia Bagels

✉ 2836 Broadway
☎ 212/222 3200

BOLIVAR £££

This Upper East Side spot draws culinary inspiration from Latin and South America in a modern hacienda-style room with adobe walls and leafy accents. Try one of the creative cocktails served in a chunky Mexican glass, and save room for the house-made chocolates in exotic flavours.
✚ F5 ✉ 206 E60th Street ☎ 212/838 0440 ◷ Daily ⊜ 4, 5, 6 59th Street

CALLE OCHO ££

Vaulted ceilings, colourful murals, and beaded curtains radiate a South American vibe while maintaining a modern, stylish New York feel. The cuisine is sophisticated enough for discerning palates yet true to its Latin American heritage.
✚ E2 ✉ 446 Columbus Avenue (81st/82nd Streets) ☎ 212/873 5025 ◷ Closed lunch ⊜ 1, 9 79th Street

MOLYVOS £££

A bustling restaurant that evokes a Greek seaside village, a feeling enhanced by the earthy tones and ancient vases. The food furthers the illusion – wild stripped bass plaki will transport you to the Aegean.
✚ E5 ✉ 871 Seventh Avenue (55th/56th Streets) ☎ 212/582 7500 ◷ Daily ⊜ N, R Seventh Avenue

PATRIA £££

'Nuevo Latino' cuisine provides astonishing combinations, bright flavours, and plenty of spice. The fried snapper and Patria pork entrées on the prix-fixe only menu pay homage to their Latin roots while becoming something completely new – much like Patria itself.
✚ D8 ✉ 250 Park Avenue South (20th Street) ☎ 212/777 6211 ◷ Closed Sun ⊜ N, R 23rd Street

PONGAL £

Come here to enjoy the fragrant vegetarian cooking of the southern regions of India. If the menu intimidates, order one of the *thalis* so you can sample several dishes. By the way, it's strictly kosher.
✚ D8 ✉ 110 Lexington Avenue (27th/28th Streets) ☎ 212/696 9458 ◷ Daily ⊜ 6 28th Street

ROSA MEXICANO £££

This perennial favourite is always a fiesta – loud, colourful and crowded. The menu consists of upmarket versions of authentic Mexican dishes and there isn't a loser on the list. Three different rooms offer various moods.
✚ G5 ✉ 1063 First Avenue (58th Street) ☎ 212/753 7407 ◷ Daily ⊜ 4, 5, 6 59th Street

TABLA £££

A grand staircase leads to the dining room accented by exotic flowers and sleek furnishings. The menu explores the intriguing flavours of India. Don't fill up on the delicious bread from the tandoor oven, save room for the many other culinary revelations.
✚ D8 ✉ 11 Madison Avenue (25th Street) ☎ 212/889 0667 ◷ Closed Sun lunch ⊜ 6 23rd Street

DINERS, DELIS & PIZZA

ARTURO'S PIZZERIA £

Don't go for the decor, or the service, and definitely don't go for quiet conversation. Go for some of the best coal-oven pizza in town, in a lively, sometimes raucous, setting. The dough is slightly thicker than the classic Neapolitan variety but the crusty pie will satisfy a pizza-lover's dream.

⊞ B10 ⊠ 106 Houston Street (Thompson Street) ☎ 212/677 3820 ⏰ Closed lunch 🚇 1, 9 Houston Street

BARNEY GREENGRASS ££

BG serves classic Jewish breakfast fare like bagels, cream cheese and the definitive smoked sturgeon. An individual *babka* (chocolate streusel danish) will take the edge off while you wait upwards of an hour for your table.

⊞ E1 ⊠ 541 Amsterdam Avenue (86th Street) ☎ 212/724 4707 ⏰ Closed Mon 🚇 1, 9 86th Street

CAFE HABANA £

Modern lunch counter with expensive and tasty Latin diner fare like Cuban sandwiches and *camarones al ajillo* (shrimp in garlic sauce). The bright blue booths and loud Latin music make it a popular choice for the hip, downtown crowd.

⊞ C10 ⊠ 17 Prince Street (Elizabeth Street) ☎ 212/625 2001 ⏰ Daily 🚇 6 Spring Street

CARNEGIE DELI ££

Mile-high sandwiches are the draw at this New York institution – one is enough to feed a small army (but beware the sharing charge). A favourite of theatre types and deli lovers; it's a place you've got to try to really experience the city.

⊞ E5 ⊠ 854 Seventh Avenue (55th Street) ☎ 212/757 2245 ⏰ Daily 🚇 N, R Seventh Avenue

KIEV £

This quintessential Eastern European diner, complete with abrupt Slavic waitresses, serves hearty food around the clock. The potato pancakes are ample and greasy, perfect with a dish of apple sauce.

⊠ 117 Second Avenue (7th Street) ☎ 212/674 4040 ⏰ Open 24 hours 🚇 6 Astor Place

LOMBARDI'S £

The aroma of thin crust pies emerging from the coal oven, red checked tablecloths, scarred tables and seasoned waitresses set the mood for some of the best pizza in Manhattan.

⊞ C10 ⊠ 32 Spring Street (Mott/Mulberry Streets) ☎ 212/941 7994 ⏰ Daily 🚇 6 Spring Street

SECOND AVENUE DELI £–££

One of the last of the real New York delis – New Yorkers who remember the good-old-days will travel across the city to feed their food cravings. A recent renovation may have removed some of the patina, but don't be fooled, it's the real thing.

⊞ D9 ⊠ 156 Second Avenue (10th Street) ☎ 212/677 0606 ⏰ Daily 🚇 6 Astor Place

Late-night munchies

There are restaurants in New York where you may have to wait for a table, even at 3AM. Late-night restaurants range from raffish dives, to chic eateries, to dark lounges, to ethnic excursions. These are some of the most popular after-hours haunts (for good reason).

Florent (24 hours)
⊠ 69 Gansvoort Street
☎ 212/989 5779

First (till 2AM)
⊠ 87 First Avenue
☎ 212/674 3823

Kang Suh (24 hours)
⊠ 1250 Broadway
☎ 212/564 6845

Corner Bistro (till 4AM)
⊠ 331 W4th Street
☎ 212/242 9502

Lansky Lounge (till 4AM)
⊠ 138 Delancey
☎ 212/677 9489

Big Nick's Pizza and Burger Joint (closed from 5–6AM)
⊠ 2175 Broadway
☎ 212/362 9238

ASIAN

Giant sushi

For the sushi connoisseur, Yama (S–SS) may not offer the best there is, but it does serve the biggest sushi and it is very good. Sadly, many people share this view, and the tiny place is engulfed with salivating sushi wolves, queuing up for hours.

+ D19 ✉ 49 Irving Place (17th Street) ☎ 212/475 0969 🕐 Closed Sun 🚇 N, R, 4, 5, 6 14th Street (Union Square)

BLUE RIBBON SUSHI £££

Terrific freshness and exotic offerings are what keeps this dark, wood-panelled sushi bar abuzz; also a very good sake selection, all of which are served in the traditional wooden boxes.

+ B10 ✉ 119 Sullivan Street (Prince/Spring Streets) ☎ 212/343 0404 🕐 Closed lunch, Mon 🚇 C, E Spring Street

BOP ££

On a deserted corner of the Bowery, Bop is an oasis of clean lines and muted tones. Upstairs are tabletop Korean barbecues emanating wonderful aromas. Other good choices are *bibimbop*, a spicy rice dish with a choice of wild mountain vegetable, or *bul go gui* (grilled shortribs).

+ C10 ✉ 325 Bowery (2nd Street) ☎ 212/254 7887 🕐 Closed lunch 🚇 F Second Avenue

KOM TANG SOOT BUL HOUSE £–££

In the middle of a block full of Korean restaurants, this bi-level emporium will offer a great taste of the cuisine. The deliciously spicy selection of *Kim chee* is the perfect primer for the tasty Korean tabletop barbecue.

+ D7 ✉ 32 W32nd Street (Fifth Avenue) ☎ 212/947 8482 🕐 Daily 🚇 B, D, N, F, R 34th Street

NEW YORK NOODLE TOWN £

A no-frills Chinatown restaurant with superb Cantonese food. Specialities include crispy baby pig, salt-baked softshell crab and, as the name implies, anything with noodles.

+ C11 ✉ 281/2 Bowery (Bayard Street) ☎ 212/349 0923 🕐 Daily 🚇 F, E Broadway

NOBU £££

It is difficult to get a reservation at this TriBeCa Japanese shrine but patience and persistance is rewarded by the hauntingly delicious cooking. The dining room is modern Japanese fantasy with lots of bamboo and rich wood tones.

+ B11 ✉ 105 Hudson Street (Franklin Street) ☎ 212/219 0500 🕐 Closed Sat, Sun lunch 🚇 1, 9 Franklin Street

REPUBLIC £

A hip restaurant on Union Square where trendy people slurp noodles while sitting at communal tables in a stylish re-creation of an Asian cafeteria. A super choice for a quick bite – the service is miraculously fast – or an evening of people-watching.

+ D9 ✉ 37 Union Square West (16th/17th Streets) ☎ 212/627 7172 🕐 Daily 🚇 4, 5, 6, N, R, L Union Square

VIET-NAM £

Don't be put off by the dingy surroundings, this basement dive serves some of the best, and cheapest, Vietnamese food in the neighbourhood with lots of choices.

+ C12 ✉ 11–13 Doyers Street (Bowery/Pell Streets) ☎ 212/693 0725 🚇 6 Canal Street

ITALIAN & MEDITERRANEAN

BARBO £££

On a quiet street right off Washington Square Park, this elegant eatery has the feel of a Roman ristorante – large marble tables, untamed flower arrangements and an informal bar area. The varied menu is based on hundreds of years of Italian tradition.

✚ C9 ✉ 110 Waverly Place (McDougal Street/Sixth Avenue) ☎ 212/777 0303 🕘 Closed lunch 🚇 A, C, E, B, D, F W4th Street

FELIDIA £££

Midtown formal Italian restaurant with an emphasis on Friulian classics. Game, pasta and risotto dishes are always expertly prepared. The impressive wine list is heavy on rare Italian selections.

✚ F5 ✉ 243 E58th Street (Second Avenue) ☎ 212/758 1479 🕘 Closed Sat, Sun lunch 🚇 59th Street

IL BUCO ££–£££

There's a festive, dinner-party feel at this unabashedly cluttered restaurant bursting with treasures from yesteryear. The Mediterranean food, such as whole orata baked in sea salt, or *stinco di vitello tartufato*, is great.

✚ C10 ✉ 47 Bond Street (Bowery/Lafayette Streets) ☎ 212/533 1932 🕘 Closed Sun, Mon lunch 🚇 6, B, F Bleecker Street

I TRULI £££

One of New York's most authentic Italian experiences. Pizzas and roasted entrées issue forth from the wood-burning oven, and all the pastas and ricotta are made in house by hand. A casual wine bar is adjacent to the main dining room.

✚ D8 ✉ 122 E27th Street (Lexington Avenue) ☎ 212/481 7372 🕘 Closed Sat lunch, Sun 🚇 6 28th Street

OSTERIA DEL CIRCO £££

This contemporary trattoria is a midtown oasis for celebrities and power brokers who'd rather not eat French all the time. The Tuscan dishes are among the best.

✚ E5 ✉ 120 W55th Street (Sixth/Seventh Avenues) ☎ 212/265 3636 🕘 Closed Sun lunch 🚇 B, D, F Rockefeller Center

SAN PIETRO £££

San Pietro is to southern Italian food what Felidia (see opposite) is to northern Italian food – a little less butter and a little more olive oil. The overall effect is sophisticated and elegant. Of particular interest are the pasta and seafood dishes.

✚ E5 ✉ 18 E54th Street (Madison Avenue) ☎ 212/753 9015 🕘 Closed Sun 🚇 E, F Fifth Avenue

SPARTINA ££–£££

Mediterranean-themed restaurant with a neighbourhood atmosphere and food that makes the trip to TriBeCa worth while. The emphasis is on Catalan cuisine. Grilled pizzas are great to nibble on while you decide what to order.

✚ A11 ✉ 355 Greenwich Street (Harrison Street) ☎ 212/274 9310 🕘 Closed Sat lunch, Sun 🚇 1, 9 Franklin Street

On the go

A slice, of pizza that is, is probably the favourite 'fast food' of New Yorkers, and indeed most neighbourhood pizzerias proffer pies that will satisfy. But New York has recently spawned a plethora of 'gourmet' fast food shops that will provide well prepared, tasty choices for those without the time for a 'real' meal.

Daily Soup

✉ 2 Rector Street
☎ 212/945 7687

Eisenberg's Sandwich Shop

✉ 174 Fifth Avenue
☎ 212/675 5096

Cosi Sandwich Bar

✉ 60 E56th Street
☎ 212/588 0888

✉ 38 E45th Street
☎ 212/949 7400

Melampo

✉ 105 Sullivan Street
☎ 212/334 9530

Mangia

✉ 16 E48th Street
☎ 212/754 7600

Peppe Rosso To-Go

✉ 149 Sullivan Street
☎ 212/677 4555

Mike's Take-Away

✉ 160 E45th Street
☎ 212/414 9661

BISTRO CHIC

Spoiled for choice?

In a city with 17,000 restaurants, there's no need for anyone to share anyone else's preferences, even if they inhabit the same block. All New Yorkers are restaurant experts, because all New Yorkers eat out more often than in (and eating in usually means ordering in). They throw dinner parties at restaurants, and they eat alone with a book at the best tables, and their repertoire includes options for both. Listings can never do justice to the depth of choice in this town.

AVENUE ££

By day this Upper West Sider serves a grazing menu of salads and delectable baked goods, plus a wonderful breakfast with fresh-baked brioche and croissants. By night it transforms into a bustling bistro that serves hearty French fare at reasonable prices.
⊞ E2 ⊠ 520 Columbus Avenue (85th Street) ☎ 212/579 3194 ⏰ Daily ⓠ 1, 9 86th Street

BALTHAZAR ££-£££

A recreated Paris brasserie, complete with red banquettes and wine choices written on the mirrored walls. The delicious food, like the seafood platters from the raw bar, keep the celebrity studded crowds coming back.
⊞ C10 ⊠ 80 Spring Street (Broadway/Crosby Street) ☎ 212/965 1414 ⏰ Daily ⓠ 6 Spring Street

BLUE RIBBON ££-£££

This small American bistro is a popular hangout for chefs and other off-duty restaurant folk. In the front window Alonso shells fresh oysters and prepares towering seafood platters. The menu offers everything from a hamburger, to foie gras, to motzoh ball soup.
⊞ B10 ⊠ 97 Sullivan Street (Prince/Spring Streets) ☎ 212/274 0404 ⏰ Closed Mon lunch ⓠ C, E Spring Street

BOUGHALEM ££

This tiny French bistro is a romantic enclave where the food is as good as the atmosphere. Nothing on the changing seasonal menu ever disappoints.
⊞ B10 ⊠ 14 Bedford Street (Sixth Avenue/Downing Street) ☎ 212/414 4764 ⏰ Closed lunch ⓠ 1, 9 Houston Street

JOJO £££

Where foodies first got a taste of New York's hottest chef, Jean-Georges Vongerichten's modern French fare. Elegantly simple food; most of the dishes are based on vegetable oils or juices rather than butter. Diners appreciate the attractive, if somewhat cramped, setting and the reasonable price tag.
⊞ F5 ⊠ 160 E64th Street (Lexington/Third Avenues) ☎ 212/223 5656 ⏰ Closed Sat lunch, Sun ⓠ 6 68th Street

PAYARD PATISSERIE AND BISTRO £££

Pastries and baked goods beckon from the showcases in this pastry shop/bistro, and the homemade chocolates and ice creams call pretty loudly, too. The bistro at the back is also worth noting.
⊞ G4 ⊠ 1032 Lexington Avenue (74th Street) ☎ 212/717 5252 ⏰ Closed Sun ⓠ 6 77th Street

SOHO STEAK ££

A compact French bistro that makes it easy to strike up conversation with your fashionable neighbours. The well prepared food, like filet mignon with potato Roquefort gallette, make this a worthy choice.
⊞ B10 ⊠ 90 Thompson Street (Prince/Spring Streets) ☎ 212/226 0602 ⏰ Closed lunch ⓠ C, E Spring Street

CLASSIC NEW YORK

CAFE DES ARTISTES £££

Howard Chandler Christy murals adorn this romantic, art-nouveau dining room, where Old-World style reigns. The menu is an appealing mix of Hungarian and French dishes ranging from sturgeon schnitzel to *pot au feu*.

✚ E3 ✉ 1 W67th Street (Central Park West/Columbus Avenue) ☎ 212/877 3500 🕐 Daily 🚇 1, 9 66th Street

FOUR SEASONS £££

Every once in a while a restaurant defines an age, and then transcends it. The Four Seasons defined the 'power lunch' and changed the face of New York dining. The dark wood-panelled Grill Room makes all diners seem like media moguls, but the romantic Pool Room makes anything seem possible. In such a grand setting the food is almost besides the point, but the seasonal menu provides many delicious options.

✚ E6 ✉ 99 E52nd Street (Park/Lexington Avenues) ☎ 212/754 9494 🕐 Closed Sat lunch, Sun 🚇 6 51st Street

PETER LUGER £££

You get steak, some hash browns and creamed spinach for the table, and maybe some tomato-and-onion salad to start– that's it, and that's all you need. It's not about atmosphere or fine wines, its not about feeling special, it's about steak. Since 1887 this landmark has been serving the best beef in New York, possibly the world.

✚ E6 ✉ 178 Broadway (Bedford Avenue) ☎ 718/387 7400 🕐 Daily 🚇 4, 6, 7 42nd Street

SPARKS £££

Vegetarians beware, you come to Sparks for the meat (and, perhaps some of the exceptional wines that line the walls of the 600-seat dining room). Every cut of beef is aged and grilled to perfection, and the double-lamb chops never disappoint.

✚ F6 ✉ 210 E46th Street (Second Avenue) ☎ 212/687 4855 🕐 Closed Sat lunch, Sun 🚇 4, 5, 6 42nd Street

'21 CLUB £££

This restaurant exudes an aura of celebrity, from the jockey that beckons at the curb, to the clubby private rooms that punctuate the townhouse setting. Known for his really expensive hamburger, Chef Erik Blauberg creates interesting dishes that feature wild game and exotic ingredients.

✚ E5 ✉ 21 W52nd Street (Fifth/Sixth Avenues) ☎ 212/582 7200 🕐 Closed Sun 🚇 B, D, F 47th–50th Streets

WINDOWS ON THE WORLD £££

The highest dining room in the country boasts a $25 million face lift and a talented new chef. The result is decent food in a comfortably retro setting. Wild Blue is a less expensive, more casual restaurant within a restaurant.

✚ A12 ✉ 1 World Trade Center (107th Floor) ☎ 212/524 7000 🕐 Closed lunch 🚇 E World Trade Center, 1, 2, 3, 9 Chambers Street

What shall we eat tonight?

When you live in New York, responses to this dilemma include: Mexican, South-western, Cajun, Southern, Italian, French, Spanish, Japanese, Chinese, Vietnamese, Caribbean, Brazilian, Cuban, Chino-Latino, Jewish, Polish, Hungarian, Ukrainian, Greek, Irish, British, Austrian, Swedish, Thai, Korean, Indonesian, Malaysian, Indian, Peruvian, Tibetan, Burmese, Ethiopian, Afghan, Lebanese or Moroccan food. Even American. In New York you soon get familiar with every national and regional cuisine, as well as most permutations of hybrid.

69

NEIGHBOURHOODS & STREETS

Born to shop

As with everything else, New Yorkers are passionate about shopping. If there is something made somewhere in the world, chances are you can buy it here – and it often sells for less than it does wherever it came from. The city has been overrun recently with so many chain stores that some avenues feel like outdoor malls. But there are still pockets of interesting, independent retailers everywhere. When a handful of shops selling similar items congregate along a street or in a neighbourhood, New Yorkers sometimes refer to the area as a 'district'. There's a flower district (W28th Street between Sixth and Seventh Avenues), a discount perfume district (E17th Street between Fifth Avenue and Union Square West), a lighting district (The Bowery north of Houston), a photography district (Flatiron side streets between Fifth and Sixth Avenues), and many more. Most of these places are set up for wholesale (trade) sales, but almost all will deal directly with the public (retail).

AVENUE OF THE AMERICAS
Superstores line the stretch between 18th and 23rd Streets (and straggle up to Macy's at 34th Street). Bargain hunt at TJ Maxx, Filene's Basement and Bed Bath and Beyond. Goodman's Treasures has an eclectic collection of home furnishings and Barnes & Noble is the store for books.
✚ C8 🚇 F 23rd Street, Path Train

CANAL STREET
The main drag of Chinatown between West Broadway and Mott Street is an irresistibly gaudy source of bogus brands: faux Gucci, Chanel, Hermès, you name it. Also gold jewellery and discounted electronics. Don't miss Pearl Paint (real art supplies and stationery) and the Pearl River Mart.
✚ B11 🚇 N, R Canal Street

ELIZABETH STREET
Centre of the chic new Nolita neighbourhood, the strip between Spring and Houston Streets is lined with tiny shops and restaurants – glass blowers, independent designers and artisanal purveyors on the cutting edge of style.
✚ C10–C11 🚇 6 Spring Street

57TH STREET
Touristy shops and theme restaurants interspersed with high fashion boutiques. Check out Chanel, Prada, Coach and Laura Ashley, then stop for a drink at the Four Seasons Hotel.
✚ D5–F5 🚇 N, R 57th Street

LOWER FIFTH AVENUE
Between 14th and 23rd Streets, Fifth Avenue has become somewhat of a mall. Gap, Banana Republic and similar shops will dress you in style, for bargains try Daffy's, and for cutting-edge women's fashions stop in Intermix. The shops lining the side streets are generally more interesting.
✚ C8–C9 🚇 N, R 23rd Street, 4, 5, 6, L Union Square

MADISON AVENUE
It doesn't get any tonier (or more expensive) than this. For clothes Versace, Armani, Valentino, or for shoes Stephane Kélian. Other notables – Crate & Barrel, Villeroy & Boch, Pierre Deux, Barneys – help to make this a shopper's haven.
✚ E6–F4 🚇 N, R Fifth Avenue

SOHO
First it was factories, then galleries, then boutiques, now chain stores – still some of the trendiest shopping anywhere. Clothing, housewares, jewellery, art, health food and more in loftlike stores.
✚ B10–C10 🚇 N, R Prince Street

UPPER FIFTH AVENUE
Worlds apart from Lower Fifth, the strip between Rockefeller Center and Central Park is home to some of the swankiest stores in town – Sak's, Bendel's, Tiffany's and Bergdorf's to name a few. Top-of-the-line jewellers include Harry Winston and Van Cleef & Arpel's.
✚ D7–F4 🚇 6 59th Street

DEPARTMENT STORES

ABC CARPET AND HOME

Organised like stores at the turn of the century (without any real 'departments') the fun at this giant home furnishings emporium is to wander the floors and to sift through the treasures. Everything is for sale, even the tables and chairs in the Parlor Cafe. The new food shop (attached to the café) is a welcome addition.

➕ D8 ✉ 888 Broadway (19th Street) ☎ 212/473 3000 🚇 4, 5, 6, L, N, R Union Square

BARNEYS

With the downtown location closed, this stylish Madison Avenue store has become the epicenter of affluent, fashion-forward New Yorkers. Designers from around the world are represented. Make-up, housewares, food and accessories are all among the finest.

➕ F5 ✉ 660 Madison Avenue (61st Street) ☎ 212/826 8900 🚇 4, 6 59th Street

BERGDORF GOODMAN

A more exclusive department store would be difficult to imagine. Women's clothing, make-up, extraordinary housewares and a lovely café are on the West side of Fifth Avenue, while menswear and haberdashery are across the street. Don't be intimidated, walk in like you own the place and the service will be superb.

➕ E5 ✉ 754, 745 Fifth Avenue (57th Street) ☎ 212/753 7300 🚇 4, 6 59th Street

BLOOMINGDALE'S

When the affluent residents of the Upper East Side need to pick something up, they look here first. In addition to clothing, furniture, linens and housewares are all top notch.

➕ F5 ✉ 1000 Third Avenue (59th Street) ☎ 212/705 2000 🚇 4, 6 59th Street

MACY'S

The sign outside says it's the largest store in the world, and by the time you've made your way across the nine block-long floors of this grandfather of all department stores, you'll believe them. Everything (including thousands of other shoppers) is here.

➕ D7 ✉ 151 W34th Street (Herald Square) ☎ 212/695 4400 🚇 B, D, F, N, R 34th Street

SAK'S FIFTH AVENUE

Trimmed in wood and decorated with majestic flora, the ground level of this shopper's paradise has the elegant air of Old New York. The boutiques on the upper floors feature exclusive designers.

➕ E6 ✉ 611 Fifth Avenue (50th Street) ☎ 212/753 4000 🚇 E, F 5th Avenue

TAKASHIMAYA

An austere Japanese aesthetic informs the atmosphere of this small but exquisite department store. Housewares and gifts are the main focus, but you'll stumble across other finds as well.

➕ E5 ✉ 693 Fifth Avenue (55th Street) ☎ 212/350 0115 🚇 E, F 5th Avenue

Pearl River Mart

You can't see this Chinese department store from the street, though it's got three floors filled with stuff and two entrances. Shop here, in an atmosphere reminiscent of some household consumer shrine of the 1950s, for chrome lunch pails with clip-on lids; embroidered silk pyjamas and Suzy Wong dresses; bamboo fans and porcelain rice bowls – all the things, in fact, you can get in the smaller Chinatown emporia, but collected under one roof. The food department sells both dried squid and English biscuits. The prices are very very low.

➕ B11 ✉ 277 Canal Street (Broadway) ☎ 212/431 4770 🚇 N, R Canal Street

CLOTHES

More shops

Agnès B
✉ 1063 Madison Avenue
☎ 212/570 9333

Armani Exchange
✉ 568 Broadway
☎ 212/431 6000

Chanel
✉ 5 E57th Street
☎ 212/355 5050

Comme des Garçons
✉ 520 W22nd Street
☎ 212/604 9200

Gianni Versace
✉ 817 Madison Avenue
☎ 212/744 6868

Gucci
✉ 685 Fifth Avenue
☎ 212/826 2600

Patagonia
✉ 101 Wooster Street
☎ 212/343 1776

Polo/Ralph Lauren
✉ 867 Madison Avenue (72nd
Street) ☎ 212/606 2100

Prada
✉ 45 E57th Street
☎ 212/308 2332

Timberland
✉ 709 Madison Avenue
☎ 212/754 0436

Yohji Yamamoto
✉ 103 Grand Street
☎ 212/966 9066

WOMEN'S

BETSY JOHNSON
This long-lived fashion darling produces fun, often outrageous, looks. (Other branches.)
✚ E3 ✉ 248 Columbus Avenue (71st Street) ☎ 212/362 3364
🚇 1, 2, 3 72nd Street

CATHERINE
Funky designer known for her cowboy hats in every colour. Also great everyday clothes in fun styles and dressier looks.
✚ B10 ✉ 468 Broome Street (Green Street) ☎ 212/925 6765 🚇 N, R Prince Street

CYNTHIA ROWLEY
Adorable, hip little dresses and shoes. The place to shop for a night out on the town.
✚ B10 ✉ 112 Wooster Street ☎ 212/334 1144 🚇 N, R Prince Street

MORGANE LE FAY
Liliana Ordas's floaty, yet tailored, slightly theatrical designs. (Branch in SoHo.)
✚ F3 ✉ 746 Madison Avenue (74th Street) ☎ 212/879 9700
🚇 6 77th Street

NICOLE MILLER
Girl-about-town Miller designs fun, fitted suits, dresses and accessories with tongue in cheek. Fabrics and finish don't always match the price tags. (Branch in SoHo.)
✚ F4 ✉ 780 Madison Avenue (66th Street) ☎ 212/288 9779
🚇 6 77th Street

MEN'S

BROOKS BROTHERS
The store that practically created the preppy look.
But can't be beat for traditional suits, shirts, casual clothes and shoes.
✚ E6 ✉ 346 Madison Avenue (45th Street) ☎ 212/682 8800
🚇 4, 6 Grand Central

CAMOUFLAGE
Casual, easy to wear styles. These are hip clothes without trying too hard.
✚ B8 ✉ 139 and 141 Eighth Avenue ☎ 212/741 5473
🚇 1, 9 18th Street

PAUL SMITH
Magnificent and expensive menswear for the fashion conscious gentleman.
✚ C8 ✉ 108 Fifth Avenue (16th Street) 🚇 4, 5, 6, N, R, L Union Street

BOTH

A.P.C.
This industrial looking space is the obvious backdrop for the simple, but ultra-chic, clothes that follow clean lines and are made of durable fabrics.
✚ C10 ✉ 131 Mercer Street ☎ 212/966 9685 🚇 N, R Prince Street

CANAL JEANS
T-shirt, plaid shirt, vintage dress, cut-offs, most brands of jeans plus Carhart and CAT workwear, and their own multi-hued cottons.
✚ C10 ✉ 504 Broadway (Broome Street) ☎ 212/226 1130 🚇 N, R Prince Street

EMPORIO ARMANI
The second label of the superstar designer provides a huge selection of wearable, somewhat pricey, clothes.
✚ C8 ✉ 110 Fifth Avenue ☎ 212/727 3240 🚇 4, 5, 6 Union Square

DISCOUNT SHOPPING

BIG STORES

CENTURY 21
This discount emporium recently added changing rooms, much to the delight of regular shoppers. You can find big-name men's and women's designers – Versace, Calvin Klein, Ralph Lauren, Romeo Gigli, Missoni – at seriously discounted prices.
✚ A12 ✉ 22 Cortlandt Street ☎ 212/227 9092 🚇 C, E World Trade Center

DAFFY'S
With some patience, and a lot of sifting through cheap imitations, you can sometimes discover some ridiculously cheap finds for men and women.
✚ C8 ✉ 111 Fifth Avenue ☎ 212/529 4477 🚇 L, N, R, 4, 6 Union Square

USED CLOTHES

ENCORE
Society-lady cast-offs can be purchased here at a fraction of the original price (which can still be hundreds of dollars). We're talking big-name designers, the kind of stuff you would wear to the Oscars. There are a few men's things for sale as well.
✚ G3 ✉ 1132 Madison Avenue ☎ 212/879 2850 🚇 6 77th Street

INA
Showroom samples and barely worn designer duds. The prices are high, but where else can you find Prada anything for under $100.
✚ C10 ✉ 101 Thompson Street (Prince Street) ☎ 212/941 4757 🚇 N, R Prince Street

KLEIN'S OF MONTICELLO
Orchard Street has long been known for bargains, but this is the best of the bunch.
✚ D11 ✉ 105 Orchard Street ☎ 212/966 1453 🚇 F Delancey Street

MICHAEL'S RESALE
Being in the middle of spiffy Madison Avenue, you'd expect quality here, and you get it – Upper East Side ladies don't buy anything without knowing its pedigree. Labels along the Ferragamo, Ungaro, Valentino axis.
✚ G3 ✉ 2nd Floor, 1041 Madison Avenue ☎ 212/737 7273 🚇 6 77th Street

OUT OF OUR CLOSET
Terin Fischer's tiny, spectacular consignment store includes current season samples from designers who make fashion fans salivate: Comme, Dolce, Mugler, Yohji, Gaultier, Chanel.
✚ C8 ✉ 136 W18th Street ☎ 212/633 6965 🚇 F 23rd Street

BROOKLYN'S DOMSEY WAREHOUSE
Bewildering acres of work clothes, military wear, jeans, prom dresses, vintage stuff sorted by era, plus a department where you pay by the pound.
✚ G14 ✉ 431 Kent Avenue/496 Wythe Avenue ☎ 718/384 6000 🚇 J Marcy Avenue

Sample sales

Many top designers – Donna Karen, French Connection, Tocca, Chaiken and Capone, Cynthia Rowley – have yearly sample sales where last season's merchandise is drastically discounted. Held in huge showrooms the amenities are severely limited and the crowds can often be daunting, but for the fashion and budget conscious they are a must. The best way to find out are through printed advertisments in magazines like *Time Out New York*, or *New York Magazine*, or on-line at www.sample.com. You may even be handed a flyer by someone in the street.

SUPERSTORES

Bigger, better

'New Yorkers don't need another boutique', the owner of the nationwaide housewares store, Crate & Barrel, declared just before his 54,000 square feet showroom opened on Madison Avenue in 1995. Regardless of whether New Yorkers agree with him, since the invasion of the superstores, it's become harder and harder for small, independent boutiques to compete. Will the big fish eat the tadpoles for lunch? It's hard to say. But why shouldn't Manhattanites enjoy up to 45 per cent discounts the rest of the country gets from superstore shopping? After all, the city's been through it all before, with no harm done. The last age of the giant department store – including S Klein's, Wanamaker's, McCreery's, Bonwit Teller and Stern Brothers of Ladies' Mile (Avenue of the Americas) – happened spookily enough, during the closing years of the last century.

BARNES AND NOBLE

In this age of illiteracy, who would have predicted book shopping would become chic? The first B&N superstore opened in 1993 – complete with café, tables, easy chairs, and a full calender of events – and quickly acquired a reputation as a singles cruising scene. The Sixth Avenue branch followed, then Astor Place and Union Square. B&N has been a New York institution since 1873. Now for many it's replaced the library.
🕂 E2 ✉ 2289 Broadway (82nd Street) ☎ 212/362 8835, and branches 🚇 1, 9 79th Street

BED, BATH & BEYOND

The first to reclaim the giant retail spaces of Sixth Avenue, this behemoth is filled with everything for the home. Oddly, the impressive stock doesn't afford much variety, but the prices are good.
🕂 C8 ✉ 620 Sixth Avenue (19th Street) ☎ 212/255 3550 🚇 F 23rd Street

COMP USA

Like a supermarket for hardware and software, this outpost of a national chain undercuts most of the competition.
🕂 D7 ✉ 420 Fifth Avenue (37th Street) ☎ 212/764 6224 🚇 B, D, F, N, R 34th Street

CRATE & BARREL

Having refreshed your wardrobe come here for the wardrobe itself, perhaps in cherrywood with cast-iron fixtures? Fashionable housewares and furniture at reasonable prices made New Yorkers adopt this national chain as their own.
🕂 F5 ✉ Madison Avenue (59th Street) ☎ 212/308 0011 🚇 N, R Fifth Avenue

NIKE TOWN NY

Enter the Spaceship Sneaker and feel like a professional athlete. High-tech videos, multilevel displays and an industrial atmosphere that encourages aerobic shopping makes this a favourite for dads and kids.
🕂 D6 ✉ 11 Pennsylvania Plaza (57th Street) ☎ 212/946 2710 🚇 N, R 57th Street

STAPLES

The 15 branches of this office supply superstore have all but forced smaller stationary shops out of business – the best prices by far. The Avenue of the Americas and Union Square stores have the largest selection.
🕂 D9 ✉ 5 Union Square West (15th Street) ☎ 212/929 6323 🚇 4, 5, 6, N, R, L Union Square; 🕂 C8 ✉ 699 Avenue of the Americas (23rd Street) ☎ 212/675 5698 🚇 F, Path, 23rd Street

TOWER RECORDS

The three branches of this New York music and entertainment warehouse attract a diverse crowd. The original on lower Broadway (which also has book and video departments) was the first and remains the favourite among die-hard fans.
🕂 C10 ✉ 692 Broadway (4th Street) ☎ 212/505 1500 🚇 B, D, F Broadway/Lafayett

FOOD

BALDUCCI'S

Comprehensive grocery beautifully laid out and irresistibly stocked with things you want to devour. This Greenwich Village shop is still owned by the family who started it as a stall across the street. The Balduccis, true to their origins, put the emphasis on Italian produce and exquisitely prepared dishes.

➕ C9 ✉ 424 Sixth Avenue (9th Street) ☎ 212/673 2600 🚇 A, B, C, D, E, F W4th Street

CHELSEA MARKET

A block-long urban gourmet shopping mall with meat, fish, baked goods, produce, restaurant supplies, wines and speciality purveyors.

➕ B8 ✉ 75 Ninth Avenue (15th Street) ☎ 212/243 6005 🚇 A, C, E 14th Street; L Eighth Avenue

DEAN & DELUCA

A loft-like space with white-washed walls, artistic displays and chic foodstuffs from around the world. Every item has its own gallery – piles of biscuits; towers of spices in tiny chrome canisters; baskets of onion ficelles; and the best (and most expensive) cheese selection in the city. A coffee bar at the entrance offers good snacks.

➕ C10 ✉ 560 Broadway (Prince Street) ☎ 212/431 8350 🚇 N, R Prince Street

GOURMET GARAGE

The place to find yellow cherry tomatoes, dried cherries, fresh clams, truffle butter, smoked duck, smoked trout, gelati, you-name-it, and it only *acts* like it's bargain-priced.

➕ B11 ✉ 435 Broome Street (Mercer Street) ☎ 212/941 5850 🚇 N, R Prince Street

GREENMARKET

Farmers travel year-round from the tri-state area to this outdoor farmers market that has rejuvenated the entire Union Square area.

➕ D9 🚇 4, 5, 6, N, R, L Union Square

KALUSTYAN'S

If it's ethnic, it's in here. Spices and exotic products from around the world are offered at bargain prices. Every foodie worth his (sea) salt knows to come here first.

➕ D8 ✉ 123 Lexington Avenue (28th Street) ☎ 212/685 3451 🚇 6 28th Street

KAM MAN

The most comprehensive Asian market, with fresh and barbecued meats, dried seafood, jarred sauces, teas, herbs and other exotica.

✉ 200 Canal Street (Mulberry Street) ☎ 212/571 0330

ZABAR'S

This is the pleasingly, wise-cracking New Yawker of the three foodie havens; bigger and more bustling than Balduci's or Dean & DeLuca, with a Jewish soul all its own. Cheese, coffee, smoked fish, breads and the like downstairs and upstairs are the city's best buys in kitchenwares.

➕ E2 ✉ 2245 Broadway (80th Street) ☎ 212/787 2000 🚇 1, 9 79th Street

Picnic spots

These don't start and end in Central Park. Some more to try, indoors and out:

Lower Manhattan Battery Park City – benches and views all along the Hudson South Street Seaport boardwalk.

SoHo The 'Vest Pocket Park' at Spring and Mulberry Streets.

Greenwich Village The ballpark at Clarkson and Hudson Streets, and St Luke's Garden at Hudson (Barrow/Grove Streets) are a well-kept secret – they're perfect!

Midtown East Greenacre Park at 51st Street and Second Avenue (what a misnomer). Crystal Pavilion at Third Avenue and 50th Street – atrium with waterfall. Paley Park (53rd Street/Fifth Avenue) – concrete canyon and waterfall.

Midtown West Equitable Tower Atrium on Seventh Avenue (51st–52nd Streets) – lots of greenery.

Upper East Side Carl Shurz Park at East End Avenue (84th–89th Streets) – Gracie Mansion, where the mayor lives, is here; also great Roosevelt Island and bridge views.

NOWHERE BUT NEW YORK

Book worms

Although the Barnes & Noble and Border's superstores claim to cover all tastes, speciality book stores abound.

Biography Book Shop If your interest lies in people's lives
✉ 400 Bleecker Street
☎ 212/807 8655

Murder Ink For mysteries and crime ✉ 2486 Broadway
☎ 212/362 8905

A Photographer's Place If you prefer looking at pictures
✉ 133 Mercer Street
☎ 212/431 9358

Hacker Art Books If fine art is your thing you can't beat this collection ✉ 45 W57th Street
☎ 212/688 7600

Books of Wonder The shelves are filled with children's books
✉ 16 W18th Street
☎ 212/989 3270

A Different Light Bookstore Gay and lesbian texts are stocked ✉ 151 W19th Street
☎ 212/989 4850
For other special interests, foreign language books, religious, scholarly or used texts, consult the Manhattan Yellow Pages.

ABRACADABRA
The largest costume and novelty shop anywhere.
🔲 C8 ✉ 19 W21st Street (Fifth Avenue) ☎ 212/627 5194
🚇 F, Path 23rd Street; N, R 23rd Street

B&H
Photography superstore with everything you need to take perfect pictures available at good prices.
🔲 C6 ✉ 420 Ninth Avenue (34th Street) ☎ 212/444 6625
🚇 A, C, E 34th Street

DOM
Eclectic collection of decidedly downtown housewares, gifts, clothes and more.
🔲 B10 ✉ 382 W Broadway (Broome Street) ☎ 212/334 5580 🚇 C, E Spring Street

ENCHANTED FOREST
Like walking into a fairy tale, this artisanal toy store will enchant adults and children alike.
🔲 C10 ✉ 85 Mercer Street
☎ 212/925 6677 🚇 N, R Prince Street

FIREFIGHTERS FRIEND
You can live out your fantasy of becoming a firefighter (or being rescued by one) at this NYFD store. T-shirts, trucks and oilskin jackets for sale.
🔲 C10 ✉ 263 Lafayette Street ☎ 212/226 3142
🚇 6 Spring Street

THE HAT SHOP
Custom-made toppers for women with a distinct downtown flair.
🔲 B10 ✉ 120 Thompson Street (Prince Street)
☎ 212/219 1445
🚇 E Spring Street

J&R
This sprawling complex of shops offers music, computers, office equipment and related products at some of the best prices in town.
🔲 B12 ✉ 15–23 Park Row (Beekman Street) ☎ 212/238 9000 🚇 2, 3 Park Place; A, C Broadway-Nassau Street; N, R, 4, 5, 6 City Hall

KATE'S PAPERIE
The beautiful handmade papers and stationery paraphernalia is overwhelming at this SoHo boutique.
🔲 C10 ✉ 561 Broadway
☎ 212/941 9816 🚇 N, R Prince Street

KIEHL'S
Exclusive handmade personal hygiene products for men and women. They give out samples of everything and the owner's collection of Harley Davidson motorcycles is on permanent display.
🔲 D9 ✉ 109 Third Avenue (13th Street) ☎ 212/677 3171
🚇 L Third Avenue

KITCHEN ARTS & LETTERS
Books for the cook and food scholar. Imports and hard-to-find cookbooks are a speciality.
🔲 H2 ✉ 1435 Lexington Avenue (94th Street)
☎ 212/876 5550 🚇 4, 5, 6 96th Street

LITTLE RICKIE'S
Novelty items through the ages – glue-on beauty marks, animal farms, wind-up teeth, greeting cards.
🔲 D10 ✉ 491/2 First Avenue (3rd Street) ☎ 212/505 6467
🚇 F Second Avenue

M.A.C.

If deep, rich, matte make-up colours are what you are looking for, you'll find them at this ultra-trendy boutique.

➕ C9 ✉ 14 Christopher Street ☎ 212/243 4150 Ⓜ A, B, C, D, E, F W4th Street

MACKENZIE-CHILDS

Picture Alice in Wonderland meets Rosenthal. Day-glo 3-D ceramics and gifts in an enchanting boutique. The expensive afternoon tea is worth it for the delicious pastries.

➕ F4 ✉ 824 Madison Avenue (69th Street) ☎ 212/570 6050 Ⓜ 6 68th Street

MAXILLA & MANDIBLE

'Dem bones, 'dem bones. Plus butterflies, antlers and shells.

➕ E2 ✉ 453 Columbus Avenue (81st Street) ☎ 212/724 6173 Ⓜ C 81st Street

MOMA DESIGN STORE

Clever design and clean lines are the emphasis at this gift outlet of the Museum of Modern Art.

➕ E5 ✉ 44 W53rd Street (Fifth Avenue) ☎ 212/767 1050 Ⓜ E, F Fifth Avenue

MXYPLYZYK

Modern urban gifts with sleek design and a sense of humour. Beautiful wrapping.

➕ D8 ✉ 125 Greenwich Avenue (12th Street) ☎ 212/989 4300 Ⓜ A, C, E 14th Street

THE NOOSE

Serious S&M fetish wear and paraphernalia for men.

➕ C8 ✉ 261 W19th Street (Eighth Avenue) ☎ 212/807 1789 Ⓜ C, E 23rd Street

PANDORA'S BOX

It's hard to move for the plaster-cast cherubs, Nefertitis, columns and Elvises.

➕ B10 ✉ 153 Prince Street ☎ 212/505 7615 Ⓜ C, E Spring Street

PEARL PAINT

Great prices and a great selection of art supplies, craft materials and all related merchandise.

➕ B11 ✉ 308 Canal Street (Broadway) ☎ 212/431 7932 Ⓜ N, R Canal Street

POP SHOP

Keith Haring's art for the masses – on umbrellas, tote bags, you name it.

➕ C10 ✉ 292 Lafayette Street (Houston Street) ☎ 212/219 2784 Ⓜ 6 Spring Street

RICHART

Retail outlet for one of France's most creative chocolatiers – beautiful designs and exotic fillings.

➕ E5 ✉ 7 E55th Street (Fifth Avenue) ☎ 212/371 9369 Ⓜ E, F Fifth Avenue

STEUBEN

Gallery/retail showroom displaying the work of America's renowned glass artists.

➕ E5 ✉ 717 Fifth Avenue (56th Street) ☎ 212/752 1441 Ⓜ E, F Fifth Avenue

TOURNEAU

Careful, you may get so caught up in the commotion at this timepiece superstore that you are tempted into overspending.

➕ E5 ✉ 590 Madison Avenue (57th Street) ☎ 212/758 7300 Ⓜ E, F Fifth Avenue

Flea markets

In New York, where everything has the potential to show up on a film set or in a designer's showroom, bric-à-brac is at a premium. The main flea market, called the Annex, runs on Saturdays and Sundays (✉ Sixth Avenue at 26th Street ☎ 212/243 5343). One section requires a small admission fee. Sifting through the antiques and junk you might brush up against the likes of Catherine Deneuve.

SoHo has a smaller market (✉ Broadway at Grand Street ☎ 212/682 2000) where the shopping and people-watching is less interesting.

Down the street from the Annex is the Garage, an multilevel indoor antiques market (✉ 112 W25th Street ☎ 212/647 0707), open only on the weekends.

Uptown check out the Sunday-only I.S. 44 Green Flea (✉ Columbus Avenue at 77th Street ☎ 212/721 0900) and the Saturday-only inside-outside P.S. 183 market (✉ E67th Street at York Avenue).

DRINKS

Drink up

Cocktail culture is alive and well in the Big Apple. The martini craze continues to gain momentum – many bars and lounges offer long menus of creative concoctions with witty names. Elegant glassware is crucial. Atmospheres range from urban chic to clubby lounge to Old New York. Neighbourhood pubs, with more emphasis on beer and scotch, are favourite watering holes. But if you'd rather stay off the hard stuff altogether, you can sit back and relax at any one of the zillion coffee bars that have recently opened around town.

URBAN CHIC

FOUR SEASONS HOTEL

I M Pei's design gives this a sleek, austere energy. Impressive martini menu and great snacks.

☐ F5 ☒ 57 E57th Street (Lexington Avenue) ☎ 212/758 5700 ⦿ 4, 5, 6 59th Street

LOT 61

Giant space with rubber couches and expensive contemporary art on the walls.

☐ B7 ☒ 550 W21st Street (Eleventh Avenue) ☎ 212/243 6555 ⦿ C, E 23rd Street

MERCER HOTEL LOBBY BAR

The friendly modelesque service at this tiny SoHo hotspot makes having a drink a pleasant, chic experience.

☐ C10 ☒ 99 Prince Street (Mercer Street) ☎ 212/966 6060 ⦿ N Prince Street

CLUBBY LOUNGES

CHEZ ES SAADA

The underground caves of this Moroccan-inspired complex feel elegantly exotic.

☐ D10 ☒ 42 E1st Street (2nd Avenue) ☎ 212/777 5617 ⦿ B, D, F, Q Lafayette

THE GREATEST BAR ON EARTH

Perched atop the World Trade Center, this lounge changes character (and clientele) every night of the week.

☐ A12 ☒ 1 World Trade Center (107th Floor) ☎ 212/524 7000 ⦿ C, E World Trade Center; 1, 2, 3, 9 Chambers Street

10TH STREET LOUNGE

Ultra-cool atmosphere with flickering cathedral candles and low couches.

☐ C10 ☒ 212 E10th Street (Second Avenue) ☎ 212/473 5252 ⦿ 6 Astor Place

NEIGHBOURHOOD PUBS

THE GINGER MAN

Friendly atmosphere with an incredible beer and scotch selection.

☐ D7 ☒ 11 E36th Street (Fifth Avenue) ☎ 212/532 3740 ⦿ N, R, B, D, F, Q 34th Street

WHITE HORSE TAVERN

Here Dylan Thomas drank his last. A picturesque village pub.

☐ B9 ☒ 567 Hudson Street ☎ 212/243 9260 ⦿ 1, 9 Christopher Street

PETE'S TAVERN

1864 Gramercy Park Victorian saloon where O Henry wrote *The Gift of the Magi*.

☐ D9 ☒ 129 E18th Street ☎ 212/473 7676 ⦿ N, R, 4, 6 Union Street

COFFEE

CAFEÉ REGGIO

The original, pre-coffee bar craze, Roman rococo, bohemian espresso house.

☐ B10 ☒ 119 McDougal Street ☎ 212/475 9557 ⦿ A, B, C, D, E, F W4th Street

SCHARMANN'S

The service is inattentive and the attitude flies, but this is a unique coffee bar with a definite SoHo feel.

☐ B10 ☒ 386 W Broadway (Broome Street) ☎ 212/219 2561 ⦿ C, E Spring Street

PERFORMANCE

BAM
The Brooklyn Academy of Music mounts major cutting-edge extravaganzas in every performing art: dance, opera, theatre, classical music, to name a few.
+ Off map at L14 **✉** 30 Lafayette Avenue, Brooklyn **☎** 718/636 4100 **⊕** A, C Lafayette Avenue

JOSEPH PAPP PUBLIC THEATER
With two stages, there is always something worth seeing. Recent successes include *Bring in da Noise, Bring in da Funk*.
+ C10 **✉** 425 Lafayette Street **☎** 212/598 7150 **⊕** B, D, F Broadway/Lafayette

THE KITCHEN
An intimate theatre for avant-garde performances. Everything from women acrobats to tragic monologues.
+ B7 **✉** 512 W19th Street (Eleventh Avenue) **☎** 212/255 5793

92ND ST Y
Cabaret, music, dance and readings are among the happenings here.
+ H2 **✉** 1396 Lexington Avenue (92nd Street) **☎** 212/996 1100 **⊕** 6 96th Street

P.S. 122
A converted school that hosts a wide range of acts from the bizarre to the poignant.
+ D10 **✉** First Avenue (9th Street) **☎** 212/477 5288 **⊕** N, R 8th Street, F Second Avenue

SYMPHONY SPACE
Story telling, readings, children's performance, music dance and lots more.
+ E1 **✉** 2537 Broadway (95th Street) **☎** 212/864 5400 **⊕** 1, 2, 3, 9 96th Street

AMATO OPERA
This hollowed-out East Village brownstone mounts full-length grand opera in miniature.
+ D10 **✉** 319 Bowery **☎** 212/228 8200 **⊕** F Second Avenue

CARNEGIE HALL
Considered one of the greatest recital halls in the world, Carnegie Hall features an eclectic programme ranging from classical artists to folk singers.
+ E5 **✉** 881 Seventh Avenue (57th Street) **☎** 212/247 7800 **⊕** N, R 57th Street; E Seventh Avenue

THE METROPOLITAN OPERA
The gala openings at this world-class opera rank among the most glamorous of the city's cultural events. Serious buffs queue up on Saturday mornings for cheap standing-room tickets. The season runs October through April.
+ D4 **✉** Lincoln Center **☎** 212/362 6000 **⊕** 1, 9 66th Street

NEW YORK CITY OPERA
The Met's next-door neighbour, the repertoire of this fine opera company incorporates a wider variety including newer works, operetta and musicals.
+ D4 **✉** Lincoln Center **☎** 212/870 5570 **⊕** 1, 9 66th Street

Seeing is believing
On any given night of the week there is more to do and see in New York than perhaps in any other city in the world. And since movies can cost upwards of $10 anyway, you may as well see something live. From the elegance of a grand opera to the excitement of avant-garde performance art, New York spectacles are world-class (even the flops). Broadway shows can be expensive, but nothing transports like a great multimillion-dollar musical or an intense performance by a drama diva. Many theatres offer discounts if you buy your tickets at the box office the day of the show or at one of the two TKTS discount ticket outlets (**✉** Times Square/47th Street), or at the base of the World Trade Center. Be sure to book tickets in advance for the most popular shows.

79

ON THE TOWN

Keeping up

One of New York's favourite pastimes is keeping up with what's going on – even if you don't get to see something, you're expected to have an opinion. To stay abreast of what's happening around town, look for extensive weekly listings in *Time Out New York*, *New York* and *The New Yorker* magazines, or the Friday and Sunday editions of *The New York Times* (available on newsstands). You can also pick up free copies of the *Village Voice* and *New York Press* newspapers in shop fronts and vestibules around town. The monthly listing in *Paper* magazine have a decidedly downtown focus.

CABARET

CAFÉ CARLYLE
This Upper East Side lounge in the elegant Carlyle Hotel is home to Bobby Short, Eartha Kitt and other jazz greats. Bemeleman's Bar next door is less expensive and requires less advanced planning.
✚ F4 ✉ Carlyle Hotel, Madison Avenue (76th Street) ☎ 212/744 1600 🚇 6 68th Street

DON'T TELL MAMMA
New names and established performers ranging from comedy to torch singers.
✚ D5 ✉ 343 W46th Street (Ninth Avenue) ☎ 212/757 0788 🚇 A, C, E 42nd Street

DUPLEX
Drag queens and downtown crooners sit around the piano bar and have a great time.
✚ B9 ✉ 61 Christopher Street (Seventh Avenue) ☎ 212/255 5438 🚇 1, 9 Christopher Street

COMEDY

CAROLINE'S COMEDY CLUB
More of the already-made-it than the up-and-coming play here, in theatreland.
✚ D5 ✉ 1626 Broadway (49th Street) ☎ 212/757 4100 🚇 1, 9 50th Street

CAROLINE'S ON BROADWAY
Established names will make you either laugh or groan.
✚ D5 ✉ 1626 Broadway (49th Street) ☎ 212/757 4100 🚇 1, 9 50th Street

GOTHAM COMEDY CLUB
Agreeable venue for up-and-coming stand-up comedians.
✚ D8 ✉ 34 W22nd Street (Fifth Avenue) ☎ 212/367 9000 🚇 N, R 23rd Street; F, Path 23rd Street

JAZZ

BLUE NOTE
Many big names come to play at this famous club. The cover is high, but the quality of the acts merits it.
✚ C9 ✉ 131 W3rd Street ☎ 212/475 8592 🚇 A, B, C, D, E, F W 4th Street

SWEET BASIL
No less serious than Blue Note, but a little less commercial, this is where the die-hards go to catch their favourite acts.
✚ B9 ✉ 88 Seventh Avenue South (Grove Street) ☎ 212/242 1785 🚇 1,9 Christopher Street

27 STANDARD
This class-A venue has earlier set times than most clubs. Excellent restaurant.
✚ D8 ✉ 116 E27th Street (Third Avenue) ☎ 212/576 2232 🚇 6 28th Street

VILLAGE VANGUARD
This basement venue is the *ne plus ultra* of divey jazz clubs. The scene is still as hot as the day it opened in 1935.
✚ B9 ✉ 178 Seventh Avenue South (11th Street) ☎ 212/255 4037 🚇 1, 9 Christopher Street

CLUBBING

MOTHER
More intimate than some of the other venues,

Tuesday night's Jackie 60 party is considered by many to be the most fun in town.

✚ B8 ✉ 432 W14th Street (Washington Street) ☎ 212/366 5680 🚇 A, C, E, 14th Street

NELL'S

Nell Campbell's two-level lounge endures, attracting all ages and types.

✚ B8 ✉ 246 W14th Street ☎ 212/675 1567 🚇 A, C, E 14th Street

S.O.B.'S

The Latin beat keeps you dancing at this tropically decorated nightclub ('Sounds of Brazil'). Also African, reggae and other island music.

✚ B10 ✉ 204 Varick Street ☎ 212/243 4940 🚇 1, 9 Canal Street

TUNNEL

The largest club operating still attracts thousands each night. Superstar DJ Junior Vasquez spins very late on Saturday night into Sunday morning.

✚ B6 ✉ 220 Twelfth Avenue (27th Street) ☎ 212/695 4682 🚇 C, E 23rd Street

TWILO

The most powerful sound-system in town shakes the rafters with industrial house and electronica.

✚ B6 ✉ 530 W27th Street (Eleventh Avenue) ☎ 212/268 1600 🚇 C, E 23rd Street

LIVE MUSIC

BEACON THEATER

Big names fill the marquee at this uptown venue – everything from disco diva Chaka Khan to retro modern rockers the Black Crowes.

✚ E2 ✉ 2124 Broadway (74th Street) ☎ 212/496 7070 🚇 1, 2, 3, 9 72nd Street

BROWNIES

Urban youth cram nose to tail into this Alphabet City standby. If the band *du jour* isn't here, try Sidewalk three blocks south.

✚ D10 ✉ 160 Avenue A (11th Street) ☎ 212/420 8392 🚇 F Second Avenue

CBGB & OMFUG

This no-frills club gave birth to punk rock and new wave and it's still going strong.

✚ C10 ✉ 315 Bowery ☎ 212/982 4052 🚇 F Second Avenue

IRVING PLAZA

You never know who might show up on the calendar for this medium-sized venue with a neighbourhood atmosphere.

✚ D9 ✉ 17 Irving Place ☎ 212/777 6800 🚇 N, R, 4, 6 Union Square

MERCURY LOUNGE

A laid-back atmosphere that borders on swank provides an intimate setting for top-notch performers.

✚ D11 ✉ 217 E Houston Street ☎ 212/260 4700 🚇 F Second Avenue

TRAMPS CAFE

Refreshingly uncramped with plenty of atmosphere that attracts a diverse rota of acts. The likes of Bruce Springsteen have been known to hop on stage.

✚ C8 ✉ 45 W21st Street ☎ 212/727 7788 🚇 F 23rd Street

Night Crawlers

Clubbing in New York is an art form. Most dance clubs don't get going until well after midnight, and some don't stop until noon the next day. Party promoters host different theme nights on different days of the week – each brings a unique crowd: young, old, gay, Latino, check weekly listing to see what's going on where. Cover charges are steep (upwards of $20 at the more popular places) and bouncers are notorious for how harshly they scrutinise the hordes waiting to get in. Being on 'the list' means you enter quickly and for free. Don't be intimidated, eventually the doors part for everyone. As a rule, Friday and Saturday nights you'll see mostly suburbanites and tourists; the die-hard New York clubbers preferring Sunday through Wednesday, when the ability to stay out all night is as much about status as it is about having fun. If the sight of people doing drugs, men wearing dresses or people wearing next to nothing at all bothers you, you should probably stay at home.

FREE SUMMER ENTERTAINMENT

Summer in the city

Although New York can be brutally hot in the summer, and the humidity makes it sticky, it does have its upside. Many New Yorkers flee the city each weekend: to timeshares in the Hamptons, Fire Island or Duchess County. This leaves the city's museums, cinemas, theatres, nightclubs, bars and restaurants relatively empty for intrepid out-of-towners to explore. But one of the best reasons to brave the summer heat is for the wonderful selection of free entertainment put on by many of the city's premier cultural institutions. Without paying a dime it's possible to enjoy al fresco operas, theatre, art, eating, jazz, classical music, films, dance, rock-and-roll, blues and folk music. Many arrive early for big performances and stake out a spot for a picnic. For events on the Great Lawn, in Central Park, the sky over the area is filled with coloured balloons that clever picnickers fly from their spots to indicate to their friends where they are.

MUSIC

CENTRAL PARK SUMMER STAGE

Fantastic free concerts. The line-up has included Tracy Chapman, David Byrne and countless other music-world luminaries.
✚ F4 ✉ Naumberg Bandshell (72nd Street) ☎ 212/360 2777 ◷ Jun–Aug 🚇 C 72nd Street

LINCOLN CENTER OUT-OF-DOORS (➤ 39)

Summer-long programme that includes, music, dance, educational activities and art.
☎ 212/872 5400

METROPOLITAN OPERA IN THE PARK

A whole season of free park concerts on the great lawn – truly a gala affair.
☎ 212/362 6000

NEW YORK PHILHARMONIC

As above.
☎ 212/721 6500 ◷ Jul–Aug

WORLD FINANCIAL CENTER (➤ 51)

The Plaza has concerts and dance performances for after-work revellers.
☎ 212/945 0505

THEATRE

SHAKESPEARE IN THE PARK

You will have to queue for tickets to experience these free world-class performance staged outdoors. Why not make a day of it and bring a picnic lunch?
✚ F2 ✉ Delacorte Theater, Central Park ☎ 212/539 8750 ◷ Jul–Aug 🚇 B, C 81st Street

HBO SUMMER FESTIVAL AT BRYANT PARK

Monday nights throughout summer movies are shown on a giant screen.
✚ D6 ☎ 212/983 4142

DANCING

MIDSUMMER NIGHT SWING

'Dances under the Stars' is the subtitle for this weekly public party.
✚ D4 ✉ Lincoln Center Plaza ☎ 212/875 5400 ◷ Jun–Jul 🚇 1, 9 66th Street

FESTIVALS

FOURTH OF JULY

Celebrations kick off at the Stars and Stripes Regatta ✉ South Street Seaport ☎ 212/669 9400 ◷ 3–4 Jul At night the New York Philharmonic plays in Central Park, with a firework finale ☎ 212/875 5030, and Macy's shoots millions of dollars into the sky over the Lower Hudson ☎ 212/494 5432. Good vantage points get very crammed; consider Brooklyn.

MUSEUM MILE FESTIVAL

Perambulate Fifth Avenue visiting museums free. The street is blocked off, giving the evening a party feel.
✚ G1–G3 ◷ Jun 6–9PM 🚇 4, 5, 6 86th Street

NINTH AVENUE INTERNATIONAL FOOD FESTIVAL

Ethnic eateries sell samples from street stands.
✚ D4–C6 ☎ 212/581 7217 ◷ 3rd weekend May, 10AM–7PM 🚇 C, E 50th Street

TAKE ME OUT TO THE BALL GAME

THE GIANTS AND THE JETS

New York's beloved football teams who both play at the same stadium. The Giants last won the Superbowl in 1991, but the Jets haven't been champions since 1969. It's difficult to get tickets, as most are used by season ticket-holders.
✉ Giants Stadium, Meadowlands
☎ 201/935 3900

METROSTARS

Though soccer is not a popular sport in the US the MetroStars are slowly building a following. Many fans are transplanted Europeans or South Americans.
✉ Giants Stadium, Meadowlands
☎ 201/460 4355

THE KNICKS

New Yorkers are fiercely loyal to this hometown basketball team. Lots of fans bring binoculars to the games, mostly to watch celebs like Spike Lee and Woody Allen, who have courtside seats.
✉ Madison Square Garden
☎ Knicks Hotline 212/465 JUMP

THE RANGERS

The city's favourite hockey team (except for Islander fans). In 1994 they ploughed through the competition to win the coveted Stanley Cup.
✉ Madison Square Garden
☎ Rangers Hotline 212/308 NYRS

THE ISLANDERS

In the 1980s the Islanders hockey team reigned, much to the joy of their (mostly Long Island) fans.
✉ Nassau Coliseum
☎ 516/888 9000

THE YANKEES

Despite talk of moving the team to Manhattan they still play in 'the house that Ruth built' in the Bronx, and Yankee Stadium is still awe inspiring. The Yankees have won more World Series championships than any other baseball team, and have truly defined what it is to be a sports dynasty.
✉ Yankee Stadium
☎ 718/293 6000 🚇 #4 161st Street

THE METS

There are Yankee fans and there are Mets fans. The Mets started playing in 1962 and won the hearts of New Yorkers with their World Series victory in 1969. Since then the city has been largely divided in their loyalties.
✉ Shea Stadium
☎ 718/507 8499

THE NEW JERSEY NETS AND THE NEW JERSEY DEVILS

Though these teams (basketball and hockey respectively) are not from New York, they play only minutes away. The closeness of the teams to New York create a 'cross-town rivalry' that is always fun for fans to follow.
✉ Continental Airlines Arena at the Meadowlands
☎ 201/935 3900

USTA NATIONAL TENNIS CENTER

This public tennis facility is also home to the US Open, where the world's tennis greats compete each year, in late August.
☎ 718/760 6200
🚇 #7 Willets Point/Shea Stadium

Outdoor activity in Central Park

Despite Manhattan's reputation as an 'asphalt jungle', Central Park is one of the most welcoming parks in the world. For those who crave physical activity there's plenty to do.

Bike Riding You can rent no frills bicycles and join the hordes cycling around the Park's six-mile loop.

Roller Blading Skate rental and lessons are available at Wollman Rink, or you can try your luck on your own. Watch out for the hills.

Ice Skating Wollman Rink hires figure skates and hockey skates and is an ice rink in winter. There's a snack bar where you can retreat when it gets too cold (☎ 212/396 1010).

Running The most popular place for running and jogging. On New Year's Eve there is an organised Midnight Run that is part costume ball, part fireworks display and part five-mile race. Runners are toasted with champagne – a great way to ring in the new year.

LUXURY HOTELS

Prices

Expect to pay the following prices per night for a double room:

Luxury	over $275
Mid-range	$120–$275
Budget	under $120

The new style of luxury

Traditionally New York's priciest hotels have offered traditional amenities in conservative, formal settings. In the last two decades however, a crop of ultra-chic hotels opened around the city that offer guests truly luxurious amenities in modern, stylish settings. The first was the Royalton, which started the trend in 1987. Then came the SoHo Grand in 1996, followed by the Mercer Hotel and the W New York in 1998. The hotels not only offer hip accommodation and grand services, but also restaurants, lounges and bars that attract trendy New Yorkers from all corners of the city.

FOUR SEASONS

Part of the luxury chain, this I M Pei designed masterpiece redefines grandeur. The soaring entrance may induce vertigo, but the lovely rooms will offer calm relief – neutral and wood tones with marble bathrooms and king sized beds. Health club.

✚ E5 ✉ 57 E57th Street
☎ 212/758 5700 🍴 5757
🚇 B, Q 57th Street

THE MARK

This exquisite and peaceful townhouse-mansion, a couple of blocks from the park on the Upper East Side, features antiques, goose-down pillows, palms, Piranesi prints and (mostly) your own kitchen.

✚ F3 ✉ 25 E77th Street
☎ 212/744 4300 🍴 Mark's
🚇 6 77th Street

MERCER HOTEL

A favourite among young celebrities the Mercer exudes downtown glamour. The elegantly spare rooms have lots of black and beige furnishings. Some deluxe rooms have an incredible deep, freestanding marble tub in the middle of the bathroom.

✚ C10 ✉ 99 Prince Street
☎ 212/966 6060 🍴 Mercer Kitchen 🚇 N, R Prince Street

ROYALTON

The modern art-deco lobby has one of the most innovative bars (guests sit on big cushions on a wide staircase or snuggle in oversized chairs). The rooms convey a similar feel, modern luxury with all the amenities.

✚ D6–E6 ✉ 44 W44th Street
☎ 212/869 4400 🍴 44
🚇 1, 2, 3, 9 Times Square

ST REGIS

Formal Louis XV style makes this a bona-fide oasis in the middle of midtown. The service is discreet and thorough, and the rooms are plush. In the famous King Cole Bar gentlemen puff cigars under a Maxfield Parrish mural. Fitness club.

✚ E5 ✉ 2 E55th Street (Fifth/Madison Avenues)
☎ 212/753 4500
🍴 Lespinasse 🚇 6 51st Street

SOHO GRAND HOTEL

In the heart of SoHo and convenient for shopping, this trendy hotel provides guests with decidedly New York amenities: Kiehl's products in the bathrooms, a gourmet mini-bar stocked by Dean & DeLuca and Frette sheets. There are unobstructed views of lower Manhattan

✚ B11 ✉ 310 W Broadway
☎ 212/965 3000 🍴 Canal House 🚇 A, C, E Canal Street

W NEW YORK

This New Age urban hotel offers luxuriously natural accommodation. The Mondrian-esque restaurant cooks all its food without added fat. All the rooms have featherbeds, custom sheets and lots of natural fibres. There is even a wheatgrass plant with a 'water me' sign in each room

✚ E6 ✉ 541 Lexington Avenue ☎ 212/755 1200
🍴 Heartbeat 🚇 6 51st Street

MID-RANGE HOTELS

THE AVALON
Boutique hotel opened in 1998 in a former office building on newly-chic lower Madison Avenue. The comfortably decorated rooms are large by New York standards. Each room comes with a 'body pillow' – a full sized pillow that guests can snuggle against in bed. Those who have tried claim to have had the best nights' sleep ever.
✚ D7 ✉ 16 E32nd Street ☎ 212/299 7000 🚇 6 33rd Street 🍴 Larry Forgione's Coach House

HOTEL BEACON
Located right in the middle of Broadway, on the Upper West Side, the Beacon feels more like an apartment building than a hotel. The rooms are large, with lots of wardrobe space and some have kitchenettes.
✚ E2 ✉ 2130 Broadway (75th Street) ☎ 212/787 1100 🚇 1, 2, 3 72nd Street

FITZPATRICK
The sole US representative of the family-owned Dublin chain, this hotel on the easterly side of midtown has the charm of the Irish in abundance. It stands out for service, good taste – and the perfect brunch.
✚ F5 ✉ 687 Lexington Avenue ☎ 212/355 0100 🍴 Fitzers 🚇 4, 6 59th Street

FRANKLIN
In the heart of Upper East Side, this lovely boutique hotel offers a luxurious setting close to the city's major museums, Central Park and premier

shopping on Madison Avenue. The small rooms are tastefully furnished and comfortable.
✚ G3 ✉ 164 E87th Street ☎ 212/369 1000 🚇 4, 5, 6 86th Street

MAYFLOWER
A classic hotel offering comfort and charm in a residential neighbourhood near Lincoln Center. Many rooms have spectacular views of Central Park. A great choice for those who would rather avoid the bustle of midtown.
✚ E4 ✉ Central Park W (61st Street) ☎ 212/265 0060 🍴 The Conservatory 🚇 A, C, D 1 59th Street

MORGAN
Ian Schraeger, the nightlife impresario responsible for Studio 54, built this sleekly designed hotel in the late 1980s. Spare rooms are decorated with black-and-white photographic prints – Mapplethorpe among them – and offer quiet and privacy.
✚ D7 ✉ 237 Madison Avenue ☎ 212/686 0300 🚇 6 33rd Street

THE RODGER WILLIAMS
Despite the name there is a Japanese motif running throughout. The rooms are spare yet comfortable with down comforters, Belgian linens, CD players and VCRs. Fresh flowers are an added special touch as is the complimentary buffet that is served throughout the day.
✚ D7 ✉ 131 Madison Avenue ☎ 212/448 7000

The Algonquin
The Algonquin is forever associated with the only group of literary wits to be named after a piece of furniture: the Algonquin Round Table. Not quite the Bloomsbury Group, the *bon viveurs* achieved almost as much at the bar here as they did in the pages of the embryo *New Yorker*, with Robert Benchley, Dorothy Parker and Alexander Woollcott particularly well ensconced. The hotel's Rose Room still contains the very table, and *The New Yorker's* offices still decant straight into the hotel.

BUDGET HOTELS

B&Bs

Those who prefer real neighbourhoods, authentic experiences and behaving like a local may opt for a B&B. Often these are found in Brooklyn brownstones, where the host has an extra room. Others are empty apartments. The only imperative is to book ahead.

Abode Bed and Breakfasts Ltd ☒ Box 20022, NY 10028 ☎ 212/472 2000

Bed and Breakfast Network of New York ☒ 134 W32nd Street, Suite 602 ☎ 212/645 8134

City Lights ☒ 450 W25th Street ☎ 212/255 1562

Inn New York ☒ 266 W71st Street ☎ 212/580 1900

New World Bed and Breakfast ☒ 150 Fifth Avenue, Suite 711 ☎ 212/675 5600

Urban Ventures ☒ Box 426, NY 10024 ☎ 212/594 5650

CARLTON ARMS

Decorated with crazy murals by artist guests, this is perhaps the wackiest hotel in New York. Amenities are minimal but there is a communal feel that makes solo travellers feel at home. As it says on the business card 'this ain't no Holiday Inn'.
➕ D8 ☒ 160 E25th Street ☎ 212/684 8337 🚇 6 23rd Street

CHELSEA SAVOY

Friendly 90-room hotel located in the heart of Chelsea. Clean, no-frills accommodation provides basic amenities. There is a complimentary Continental breakfast served each morning.
➕ C8 ☎ 212/929 9353 🚇 1,9 23rd Street

EXCELSIOR

Overlooking the Museum of Natural History this incongruous budget hotel is in a faded but still majestic, pre-war building. The rooms are bright, clean and well-maintained, and they all have kitchenettes.
➕ E2 ☒ 45 W81st Street ☎ 212/362 9200 🍴 Coffee shop 🚇 B, C 81st Street

GERSHWIN

'We're just at the edge of hip', says the manager of this first New York Interclub hotel–Urs Jakob's string of superhostels. Art elevates the style of basic rooms; and bars, roofdecks and lounges encourage sociability.
➕ D8 ☒ 7 E27th Street ☎ 212/545 8000 🍴 Café 🚇 N, R 23rd Street

MALIBU

A step above a youth hostel; you can get ridiculously cheap single rooms, with shared bath. Otherwise the rooms are comfortable, if bare, and there are no phones.
➕ Off map ☒ 2688 Broadway ☎ 212/222 2954 🚇 1,9 103rd Street

OFF SOHO SUITES

Located in the Lower East Side, which in recent years has been transformed to the centre for hip, downtown grunge. For those that want to rub shoulders with young, arty types (piercings and tattoos abound) this is the place. Rooms are generously sized, even if the decor is somewhat garish.
➕ C11 ☒ 11 Rivington Street ☎ 212/979 9808 🍴 Le Gourmet Deli; SoHo Suites Café 🚇 F Second Avenue

SEAPORT INN

Part of the Best Western chain, this budget hotel offers predictable comfort. Uniquely located near the South Street Seaport, with easy access to lower Manhattan.
➕ B12 ☒ 33 Peck Slip ☎ 212/766 6600 🚇 2, 3, 4 Fulton Street

WASHINGTON SQUARE

Overlooking Washington Square Park, this is the only hotel in the heart of Greenwich Village. Despite the recent renovation, the amenities are still minimal.
➕ C9 ☒ 103 Waverley Place ☎ 212/777 9515 🍴 CIII 🚇 1, 9 Christopher Street

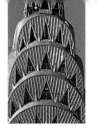

NEW YORK
travel facts

ARRIVING & DEPARTING

Before you go

- All visitors to the United States must have a valid full passport and a return ticket. For countries participating in the Visa Waiver Program, a visa is not required, though you must fill out the green visa-waiver form issued on the plane. You are also required to fill out a customs form and an immigration form.

When to go

- The New York winter can be severe, with heavy snow, biting winds and sub-freezing temperatures from December to February. It can be an ordeal to get around.
- Spring is unpredictable – even in April, snow showers can alternate with 'shirtsleeves' temperatures – but the worst of winter is over by mid-March.
- Outdoor events start in earnest in May.
- July and August are extremely hot and humid (with occasional heavy rain), driving many New Yorkers out of town. However, during this time queues are shorter, restaurant reservations optional, outdoor festivals at their peak, and the city seems rather exotic. Air-conditioning is universal, which helps.
- Autumn (fall) is generally thought the best time to visit. Warm temperatures persist into October (even November), with humidity dropping off in September.
- Average temperatures:
  Dec–Feb -2–6°C (29–43°F)
  Mar 1–8°C (34–47°F)
  Apr 7–16°C (45–61°F)
  May 12–21°C (54–70°F)
  Jun 17–27°C (63–81°F)
  Jul–Aug 20–32°C (68–90°F)
  Sep 16–24°C (61–76°F)
  Oct 11–19°C (52–67°F)
  Nov 6–13°C (43–56°F)

Arriving by air

- Most international flights arrive at JFK airport in Queens, about 15 miles east of Manhattan. Fewer arrive at Newark, New Jersey, 16 miles west. Domestic flights arrive at La Guardia, Queens, 8 miles east.

JFK

- Taxi: $30, plus tolls and tip. Take only a licensed cab from the official ranks.
- Bus: Carey Airport Express Coach ☎ 718/632 0500, to six stops in Manhattan about every 30 minutes; Gray Line Air Shuttle ☎ 212/757 6840 shared minibus to any location.
- Helicopter: Helicopter Flight Services ☎ 212/355 0801, about $600 into the 34th Street heliport for up to four people.

Newark

- Taxi: $45–$50, plus tolls and tip.
- Bus: Carey Airport Express, see above; NJ Transit Airport Express 300 ☎ 201/762 5100, to the Port Authority every 15 minutes; Olympia Trails Airport Express ☎ 212/964 6233 to Penn Station, Grand Central and WTC every 20 minutes; Gray Line, as above.

Arriving by sea

- The *QE2* still sails into the Passenger Ship Terminal ✉ Twelfth Avenue (50th–52nd Streets)

Arriving by train

- Commuter trains (Metro-North) use Grand Central Terminal ✉ 42nd Street (Park Avenue) ☎ 212/532 4900. Long-distance trains (AMTRAK) arrive at Pennsylvania

Railroad Station ✉ 31st Street (Eighth Avenue) ☎ 212/582 6875. PATH trains from the suburbs stop at several stations in Manhattan.

Arriving by bus

• Long-distance (Greyhound) and commuter buses arrive at the Port Authority Terminal ✉ 42nd Street (Eighth Avenue) ☎ 212/564 8484

Customs regulations

• Non-US citizens may import duty free: 1 quart (32fl oz) alcohol, 200 cigarettes or 50 cigars, and up to $100 worth of gifts.
• Among restricted items for import are meat, fruit, plants, seeds and lottery tickets.

ESSENTIAL FACTS

Travel insurance

• It is essential to have adequate insurance coverage when travelling in the US, mainly because of the astronomical cost of medical procedures.
• A minimum of $1 million medical coverage is recommended.
• Choose a policy which also includes trip cancellation, baggage and document loss.

Opening hours

• Banks: Mon–Fri 9–3 or 3:30; some open longer, and on Saturday.
• Shops: Mon–Sat 10–6; many are open far later, and on Sunday; those in the Village and SoHo open and close later.
• Museums: hours vary, but Monday is the most common closing day.
• Post offices: generally Mon–Fri 10–5 or 6.
• Of course, in the city that never sleeps, you'll find much open round the clock.

National holidays

• 1 January; third Monday in January (Martin Luther King Day); third Monday in February (Presidents' Day); Good Friday (half day); Easter Monday; last Monday in May (Memorial Day); 4 July (Independence Day); first Monday in September (Labor Day); second Monday in October (Columbus Day); 11 November (Veterans' Day); fourth Thursday in November (Thanksgiving Day); 25 December.

Money matters

• The unit of currency is the dollar (= 100 cents). Notes (bills) come in denominations of $1, $5, $10, $20, $50 and $100; coins are 25¢ (a quarter), 10¢ (a dime), 5¢ (a nickel) and 1¢ (a penny, increasingly optional).
• Nearly all banks have Automatic Teller Machines (ATMs), which accept cards registered in other countries that are linked to the Cirrus or Plus networks. Before leaving home, check which network your cards are linked to, and ensure your personal identification number is valid in the US. Check also on frequency limits for withdrawals. Many delis and other stores in New York have ATMs that give cash to most card types, though these charge a transaction fee (usually $2).
• Credit cards are also a widely accepted and secure alternative to cash.
• US-dollar traveller's cheques function like cash in all but small shops; $20 and $50 denominations are the most useful. Don't bother trying to exchange these (or foreign currency) at the bank – it is more trouble than it's worth, and commissions are high.

Etiquette

- Tipping: waiters get 15–20 per cent (roughly double the 8.25 per cent sales tax at the bottom of the bill); so do taxi-drivers. Bartenders get about the same (though less than $1 is mean), and will probably 'buy' you a drink if you're there a while. Bellboys ($1 per bag), room service waiters (10 per cent), and hairdressers (15–20 per cent) should also be tipped.
- Panhandlers: you will need to evolve a strategy for distributing change to the panhandlers among New York's immense homeless population. Some New Yorkers give once a day; some carry pockets of pennies; some give food; others give nothing on the street, but contribute a sum to a homelessness charity.
- Smoking is no longer a matter of politeness: there are ever more stringent smoking laws in New York. Smoking is banned on all public transport, in taxis, offices, shops and in restaurants seating more than 35.

Safety

- As in any big city, maintain an awareness of your surroundings and of other people, and try to look as if you know your way around.
- Do not get involved with street crazies, however entertaining they may seem.
- Although New York has never been safer, the less populated subway lines are probably best avoided at night, and also Alphabet City east of Avenue C, the far west of Midtown and north of about 90th Street.
- Central Park is a no-go area after dark (except for performances), and the Financial District is eerily deserted – it's best to avoid deserted places after dark.

- Apart from this, common-sense rules apply: conceal your wallet; keep the zip or clasp of your bag on the inside; and do not flash large amounts of cash, gold and diamonds, etc.

Women travellers

- New York women are street-wise and outspoken, so if someone's harrassing you, tell him to get lost – he'll be expecting it.

Places of worship

- Baptist: Memorial Baptist Church ✉ 141 W 115th Street ☎ 212/663 8830; tourists are welcomed (for a moderate charge) Sundays 10:45AM.
- Episcopal: Cathedral of St John the Divine ✉ 112th Street (Amsterdam Avenue) ☎ 212/316 7400; services at 8, 9, 11AM, 7PM. Grace Church ✉ 802 Broadway (10th Street) ☎ 212/254 2000; services at 9 and 11AM.
- Jewish: Temple Emanu-El ✉ 1 E 65th Street ☎ 212/744 1400; services at 5:30PM.
- Methodist: Christ Church United Methodist ✉ Park Avenue (60th Street) ☎ 212/838 3036; services 9 and 11AM.
- Roman Catholic: St Patrick's Cathedral ✉ Fifth Avenue (50th Street) ☎ 212/753 2261

Students

- An International Student Identity Card (ISIC) is good for reduced admission to many museums, theatres, tours and other attractions.
- Carry the ISIC or some other photo ID card at all times to prove you're over 21 if you're ' carded', or you could be denied admission to nightclubs or forbidden to buy alcohol.
- Under-25s will find it hard to hire a car.

Time differences

- New York is on Eastern Standard Time: -5 hours from the UK, -6 hours from the rest of Europe.

Toilets

- Don't use public toilets (restrooms) on the street, in stations or subways.
- Public buildings provide locked bathrooms (ask the doorman, cashier or receptionist for the key), or use those in hotel lobbies, bars, department stores or restaurants.

Electricity

- American current is 110–120 volts AC, so many European appliances need transformers as well as adapters. Wall outlets (sockets) take two-prong flat-pin plugs.

PUBLIC TRANSPORT

Subway

- New York's subway system has 469 stations, many open 24 hours (those with a green globe outside are always staffed).
- Since the recent major clean-up, carriages are free of those famous dangerous-looking graffiti and are air-conditioned. Still, the system is confusing at first, and you will probably manage some mistakes.
- To use the subway, you need a $1.50 token Metrocard, which you can refill. Unlimited ride Metrocards are also available. Drop the token or swipe the card to enter the turnstile; accompanying children under 44in tall ride free.
- Many stations have separate entrances for up- and downtown service, so ensure you're going the right way.
- Check that you are not about to get on a restricted-stop Express train that's going to whisk you to Brooklyn or the Bronx. Instead, take a 'Local' (a 'Brooklyn Bound Local' is a downtown-bound train stopping at all stations).
- If you ride at night, stay in the 'Off Hour Waiting Area' until your train arrives, then use the carriage with the conductor, in the middle of the train.
- Transit information ☎ 718/330 1234 🕑 6AM–9PM

Bus

- Buses are safe, clean – and excruciatingly slow. The fastest are Limited Stop buses.
- Bus stops are on or near corners, marked by a sign and a yellow painted kerb.
- Any length of ride costs the same as the subway, and you can use a token, a Metrocard or the correct change, which you deposit on boarding next to the driver. Ask the driver for a transfer which entitles you to a free onward or crosstown journey for an hour after boarding using the intersecting services listed on the back.
- A bus map showing many of the 200 routes travelled by the 3,700 blue and white buses is available from token-booth clerks in subway stations, and is an essential accessory.

Taxis

- A yellow cab is available when the central number (not the 'Off Duty' side lights) on the roof is lit.
- All taxis display the current rates on the door, have a meter inside, and can supply a printed receipt.
- Drivers are notorious for (a) knowing nothing about New York geography, (b) not speaking English and (c) having an improvisational driving style.

- Tip 15 per cent. Notes larger than $10 are unpopular for short journeys.

MEDIA & COMMUNICATIONS

Telephones

- Public payphones are everywhere, and they nearly always work.
- Insert a 25¢ coin, after lifting the receiver and before dialling, to pay for a five-minute local call; an additional nickel or dime is requested at the end of that time.
- Most businesses have a toll-free 800 number, and practically all also have some version of touch-tone operated phone-answering computer, which is self-explanatory.
- To dial outside the 212 area, including 800 numbers, prefix the code with a '1'.
- Hotels may levy hefty surcharges, even on local calls, so use payphones instead or the long-distance services of AT&T, MCI and Sprint that let you avoid the surcharges.
- Prepaid phonecards were starting to become available at press time, and there are a few credit card phones.

Post offices

- The main post office ✉ Eighth Avenue (33th Street) ☎ 212/967 8585 is open 24 hours. Branches are listed in the Yellow Pages 🕐 Mon–Fri 8–6, Sat 8–1
- Stamps are also available from hotel concierges and vending machines in stores, for a 25 per cent surcharge.
- Post letters in the blue metal mailboxes, or in the slots in office lobbies, air, train and bus terminals, or at post offices.

Newspapers

- The local papers are the broadsheet *New York Times* (with a huge Sunday edition) and the tabloids: the *Daily News* (also with a generously supplemented Sunday edition) and the *New York Post*. Also look for the respected *Wall Street Journal* and the pink-hued, gossip-heavy, weekly *New York Observer*.

Magazines

- As well as the *New Yorker*, *New York* and *Time Out*, you may also see the self-consciously hip *The Paper*, the glossy *Manhattan File* and the even glossier *Avenue*.

Radio

- New York's excellent National Public Radio station, WNYC, broadcasts classical and avant-garde music, jazz, news and cultural programming on FM 93.9 and AM 820.
- New York, like most US cities, is the home of the 'shock jocks' of talk radio. The most famous is Howard Stern, who broadcasts Mon–Fri 6–10AM on FM 92.3 WXRK.

Television

- Hotels usually receive most of the 93 channels available to cable subscribers at last count. 'Main stream' TV includes the national networks and cable stations, the Public Broadcasting Service and the premium cable channels, such as MTV, E! and CNN.
- In addition, there are bizarre Manhattan access channels, culture from the City University of New York (CUNY), New York 1 (with its constant onscreen weather update) and plenty of home shopping, as well as the live drama of Court TV.

International newsagents

- Many newsstands sell foreign newspapers; Hotalings ✉ 142 W 42nd Street ☎ 212/840 1868 is particularly well stocked.

EMERGENCIES

Lost property

- Be realistic – you are unlikely to recover something you lose, but try the following:
  subway and bus ☎ 718/625 6200; taxi ☎ 212/840 4734; JFK airport ☎ 718/656 4120; Newark airport ☎ 201/961 2230

Medical treatment

- If you are unfortunate enough to need medical attention, you will be extremely thankful you took out adequate insurance. Any medical practitioner will ask for your insurance papers and/or a credit card or cash payment, and medical care is very expensive.
- In the event of an emergency, the 911 operator will send an ambulance. If you have more time in hand, you may opt for a private hospital rather than the overtaxed city-owned ones.
- The Doctors on Call service ☎ 212/737 2333 is 24 hour.
- Dental Emergency Service ☎ 212/679 3966, after 8 PM 212/679 4172

Medicines

- Bring a prescription or doctor's certificate for any medications, in case of customs enquiries, as well as in the case of loss. Many drugs sold over the counter in Europe are prescription-only in the US.
- Pharmacies open 24 hours include Duane Reade ✉ 485 Lexington Avenue (47th Street) ☎ 212/682 5338; ✉ 224 W57th Street (Broadway) ☎ 212/541 9708

Emergency phone numbers

- Police, Fire Department, Ambulance ☎ 911
- Police, Fire Department, Ambulance for the deaf ☎ 800/342 4357
- Crime Victims Hotline ☎ 212/577 7777
- Sex Crimes Report Line ☎ 212/267 7273

Consulates

- Australia ✉ 636 Fifth Avenue ☎ 212/245 4000
- Canada ✉ 1251 Sixth Avenue ☎ 212/586 2400
- Denmark ✉ 825 Third Avenue ☎ 212/223 4545
- France ✉ 934 Fifth Avenue ☎ 212/606 3600
- Germany ✉ 460 Park Avenue ☎ 212/308 8700
- Ireland ✉ 515 Madison Avenue ☎ 212/319 2555
- Italy ✉ 690 Park Avenue ☎ 212/737 9100
- Netherlands ✉ 1 Rockefeller Plaza ☎ 212/249 1429
- Norway ✉ 825 Third Avenue ☎ 212/421 7333
- Sweden ✉ Dag Hammarskjøld Plaza ☎ 212/751 5900
- UK ✉ 845 Third Avenue ☎ 212/752 8400

TOURIST OFFICES

- The New York Convention & Visitors' Bureau provides free bus and subway maps, an up-to-date calendar of events. ✉ 810 Seventh Avenue, 3rd floor ☎ 212/484 1200 ◷ Mon–Fri 9–6; weekends 10–3
- The New York Division of Tourism ✉ 1 Commerce Plaza, Albany, New York N.Y 12245 ☎ 518/474 4116 or 800/225 5697 offers a free series of 'I Love New York' booklets listing attractions and a variety of tour packages.

93

Index

CityPack
New York

Written by   Kate Sekules
Edited, designed and produced by
     AA Publishing
Maps   © The Automobile Association 1996, 1999
Fold-out map © RV Reise- und Verkehrsverlag Munich · Stuttgart
     © Cartography: GeoData

Distributed in the United Kingdom by AA Publishing, Norfolk House, Priestley Road, Basingstoke, Hampshire, RG24 9NY.

The contents of this publication are believed correct at the time of printing. Nevertheless, the publishers cannot be held responsible for any errors or omissions or for changes in the details given in this guide or for the consequences of any reliance on the information provided by the same. Assessments of attractions, hotels, restaurants and so forth are based upon the author's own personal experience and, therefore, descriptions given in this guide necessarily contain an element of subjective opinion which may not reflect the publishers' opinion or dictate a reader's own experiences on another occasion.

We have tried to ensure accuracy in this guide, but things do change and we would be grateful if readers would advise us of any inaccuracies they may encounter.

A CIP catalogue record for this book is available from the British Library.

ISBN 0 7495 2219 4

Published by AA Publishing (a trading name of Automobile Association Developments Limited, whose registered office is Norfolk House, Priestley Road, Basingstoke, Hampshire RG24 9NY. Registered number 1878835).

Colour separation by Daylight Colour Art Pte Ltd, Singapore
Printed and bound by Dai Nippon Printing Co (Hong Kong) Ltd

Acknowledgements
The Automobile Association would like to thank the following photographers, picture libraries and associations for their help in the preparation of this book: Allsport UK Ltd 47a (D Strohueyer), 47b (O Greule); The Frick Collection 41b; The Mansell Collection Ltd 12; New York Convention & Visitors' Bureau, Inc 60; Rex Features Ltd 9; E Rooney 59.

The remaining pictures are held in the Association's own library (AA Photo Library) with contributions from: D Corrance 2, 6, 13a, 15, 16, 19, 21, 27b, 29a, 30, 33b, 35a, 40, 44a, 44b, 51, 52, 53; R G Elliott 1, 5b, 17, 20, 24a, 26, 27a, 28, 32, 34, 35b, 37a, 38a, 41a, 42, 43a, 43b, 45, 46, 49a, 55, 61b, 87a; P Kenward 5a, 7, 13b, 18, 23a, 23b, 24b, 25, 29b, 31a, 31b, 33a, 36, 37b, 38b, 39, 48, 49b, 50, 56, 57, 58, 61a, 87b.

Cover photographs
Main picture: Robert Harding Picture Library
Insets: Spectrum Colour Library; Zefa Pictures Ltd

THIRD EDITION UPDATED BY *KATE SEKULES*
'WHERE TO...' UPDATED BY *THE JAMES BEARD FOUNDATION*

Titles in the CityPack series
- Amsterdam - Atlanta - Bangkok - Barcelona - Beijing - Berlin - Boston -
- Brussels & Bruges - Chicago - Dublin - Florence - Hong Kong - Istanbul -
- Lisbon - London - Los Angeles - Madrid - Miami - Montréal - Moscow -
- Munich - New York - Paris - Prague - Rome - San Francisco - Seattle -
- Shanghai - Singapore - Sydney - Tokyo - Toronto - Venice - Vienna -
- Washington -